THE COLLABORATIVE DIVORCE ADVANTAGE

*Divorce Consciously to Protect Your Children &
Avoid Financial and Emotional Bankruptcy*

Kevin J. Chroman, Esq.
John C. Hoelle, JD & Peter M. Fabish, JD, MA
Kevin R. Worthley, CFP®, CDFA™
William M. Morris, CDFA™
Ria Severance, LMFT
Dominique Walmsley, MA, LMHC

MOGULY MEDIA
WALNUT, CA

Interviewer for Chapter One content: Jeremy Kossen.

Moguly Media LLC
340 S Lemon Ave, #9157
Walnut, CA 91789

www.mogulymedia.com

The Collaborative Divorce Advantage / Moguly Media, LLC. -- 1st ed.

ISBN 978-0692893425

DEDICATION

To my mentors who helped me find my path down a road less travelled. It has made all the difference. To my students, who always teach me something new, and will provide a future that is based in thoughtfulness. And, to my wife and children who provide me with constant perspective. I love you.
(Kevin J. Chroman)

Dedicated to families everywhere.
(John C. Hoelle & Peter M. Fabish)

To all who emerge from the darkness of divorce, reborn in the light of a new future.
(Kevin R. Worthley)

Dedicated to the Community Mediation Center of Knoxville, TN, whose staff work tirelessly to provide closure for families in conflict without regard to their ability to pay.
(William M. Morris)

To my children and teachers, Maia and Milan Mossé – for challenging my growth, and for being kind, loving and dedicated to sharing their ample gifts with humankind, and to my devoted mother, Marta Stern, for life-long edits, her generosity of heart, her commitment to advocate for those with less access to power, and her willingness to take on the challenge to grow at every stage of her life.
(Ria Severance)

To my children who show me and share with me the desire for deep love.
(Dominique Walmsley)

CONTENTS

PRAISE

"In my 27-year experience with Collaborative Practice, *The Collaborative Divorce Advantage* has the best treatment of process choice, financial, child specialist and divorce coach descriptions I have seen. Buy or steal this book and give it to every divorce practitioner and potential or current client."

— **Stu Webb**, Founder of Collaborative Law

"This is a tremendous go-to guide for parents who want to do divorce differently. As a lawyer and a divorced mom of two sons, I wish I had a resource like this going through my divorce and the wisdom of these practitioners to guide us to a common vision when emotions ran high. There is no substitute for a caring team. This book will help you identify the kinds of practitioners you may want to help your family through this process — and the core values you will stick to during one of the most important transitions of life."

— **Martha J. Hartney**, Attorney and Counselor at Law, CEO of Children's Emergency Response Plan (CHERP) www.gocherp.com

"If you're even thinking about divorce . . . read this book! You'll discover how a Collaborative Team will help you reach agreements that benefit you, your children, your partner, your wallet, your sanity and the quality of your co-parenting for years to come."

— **Hal Bartholomew**, JD & Founding President of Collaborative Practice California (cpcal.org) www.divorcewithrespect.com

"This book puts decency, practicality, and humanity back into the very sad, but common process of divorce. Too often, divorce is a vehicle for anger, self-righteousness, and vindictiveness. The enormous costs are born by former spouses, and their children, friends and families. Read and digest this book if you or your spouse are not getting along, have contemplated divorce or even never considered divorce. It will save you heartache, money, and self-respect, and protect your children from unnecessary emotional hardship."

— **Dr. Alan E. Fruzzetti**, international DBT expert, researcher and speaker, Author of *The High Conflict Couple: A Dialectical Behavior Therapy Guide to Finding Peace, Intimacy and Validation*

"The Collaborative Divorce Advantage is an extremely useful read for couples who have reached the mutually shared conclusion that their marriage should end. This concise and insightful collection of essays by collaborative attorneys, mediators, certified divorce financial analysts, and licensed family therapists points out the risks and costs of traditional adversarial divorce litigation and illuminates a better path through the divorce minefield."

— **Bruce I. Kogan**, Esq., Professor of Law and Mediator, Roger Williams University School of Law, Co-Founder and Past President – Rhode Island Mediators Association

"The Collaborative Divorce Advantage explains in a straightforward and wise manner how to divorce successfully. The writing is friendly and clear — so many complex questions are seamlessly answered. Our communities would be healthier if this simple material were more universally adopted."

— **Frederic Luskin**, Ph.D., Author of *Forgive for Good*

"This excellent compilation of easy to read articles makes a great case for the collaborative approach to divorce in almost any situation. Moreover, the individual perspectives from professionals ranging from divorce lawyers to financial planners to child experts to coaches provide detailed and step-by-step ways that separating parents can hire professionals to work as a team to achieve fair and lasting settlements that enable each of them to move on with their lives."

— **Alan Alhadeff**, Alhadeff & Forbes Mediation Services, Seattle, WA

"I strongly recommend *The Collaborative Divorce Advantage* to anyone wanting to spare their family the pain and cost of the standard litigated divorce in family court. This book is a short course in how to divorce collaboratively, including helpful guidance regarding finances, co-parenting and the emotional aspects of divorce."

— **Bill Eddy** Family lawyer, therapist and mediator. Developer of the *New Ways for Families*® skills training method and the Author of several books, including *High Conflict People in Legal Disputes* www.NewWays4Families.com

"The Collaborative Divorce Advantage is a long overdue and enormously valuable resource for anyone embarking on the road to divorce. The authors shed much-needed light on the various options and resources available to a divorcing couple and bring a refreshing clarity to a tumultuous and often complex process. If you know anyone contemplating or starting the divorce process, please do them a favor and give them this book."

— **Kim West**, Divorce Coach, JD, MBA, When It's Knot Forever www.whenitsknotforever.com

"The authors bring to light the dignity, humanity, and strengths of the Collaborative Divorce Process in this engaging and informative book — an easy read with valuable information for anyone entering the life-changing transition of divorce."

— **Vicki Carpel-Miller**, Collaborative Professional and Trainer, Co-Author of *Just Stop!* series, *Secondhand Shock: Surviving and Overcoming Vicarious Trauma & Secondhand Shock Workbook.*

"This is a great book that is full of insightful information and scenarios based around Collaborative Divorce. It is not only an informative resource for divorcing couples, but a relevant source to other professionals who are either directly or indirectly involved with individuals going through a divorce."

— **Laura Gustafson**, CFP®, CLU, ChFC Adjunct Faculty at Rhode Island College for graduate-level course *The Legal and Tax Issues of Marriage, Separation, and Divorce.*

"I highly recommend this book to anyone considering a divorce and to family professionals! *The Collaborative Divorce Advantage* directly and concisely gives you what you need to make an informed choice about when and why to choose Collaborative Divorce or Mediation, and how to successfully navigate the process."

— **Forrest (Woody) Mosten,** Family Law Specialist and Mediator, Los Angeles and Adjunct Professor of Law, UCLA. Author of *Collaborative Law Handbook* (Wiley, 2009), *Building a Successful Collaborative Practice* (ABA, 2018 Forthcoming), *Complete Guide to Mediation* (2015, ABA), *Mediation Career Guide* (Wiley, 2001), and *Family Lawyer's Guide to Unbundled Legal Services* (ABA, 2017, Forthcoming).

The Collaborative Divorce Advantage offers wise counsel and a truly adult approach to ending a marriage or long-term relationship, especially when children are involved. A must-read for divorcing couples and therapists on the front lines with couples contemplating divorce.

— **Judith Stevens-Long**, Ph.D., Malcolm Knowles Chair in Adult Learning and Development at Fielding Graduate University, Santa Barbara; Author of *Adult Life: Developmental Processes.*

"Historically and still, in too many countries, women do not have the option to choose their partners, let alone divorce in a respectful way that considers the well-being of all family members, with a protective net cast around the children throughout the transition. This is a trailblazing, important, must-read guide to creating workability for co-parents exiting a marriage that no longer works."

— **Ellen Snortland**, lawyer, women's rights activist, filmmaker and Author of *Beauty Bites Beast: The Missing Conversation About Ending Violence* www.beautybitesbeast.com

"This book provides a good overview for couples who view their pending divorce as an opportunity to create a positive new future for themselves (jointly) and their children. It highlights what is possible when divorcing individuals share the same goals and each genuinely desires an outcome that honors the other."

— **Kristy Larch**, Attorney at Law

"A wise and savvy guide to divorce that empowers couples to own the process and costs, honor their children, and live a better life post-divorce. Buy this book at the very least, for the sake of your children, if you are divorcing."

— **Stuart Motola**, M.A., Certified Life Coach & Author www.stuartmotola.com

"These authors have truly made their mark putting Collaborative Practice and Mediation at the top of the legal mountain for families. From cover to cover, an innovative and insightful must-read for all divorcing couples and the therapists serving them. The authors successfully challenge divorcing couples as well as divorce professionals to segue from litigation towards the world of Collaborative Divorce and Mediation."

— **Fred Glassman**, family law attorney, advocate for Collaborative Practice for decades, author of countless published articles on the subject, past President of Collaborative Practice California (CPCal) & Los Angeles County Family Law Association (LACFLA), recipient of numerous awards for his preeminent Collaborative Legal work fglawcorp.com/attorneys/glassman

"This book is a must-read for everyone considering divorce! As an advocate for women and children, and Executive Director of a nonprofit, I have witnessed the damaging fallout of an adversarial, litigated divorce — parents and children are often scarred for life. Collaborative Divorce is a humane, game-changing way to transition families through divorce, and represents a paradigm shift in our culture's compassion for divorcing families. Kudos to all the authors for this fact-filled, easy-to-read, difference-making book!"

— **Pauline Field**, Business Consultant and Author of *Feisty & Fearless: Nice Girls CAN Be Leaders*

"Don't miss reading this small gem if you want a constructive divorce that lays the groundwork for loving parenting, and the healthy co-parenting of your children as you move forward!"

— **Paul Ross**, best-selling Author of *How to Profit from Your Divorce*, shares how to put family and children unconditionally first. www.Paul-Ross.com

"If you are considering divorce, read this book. You will learn why working with your spouse is in everyone's best interests. You will see how to do your work and what support is available."

— **Ginger Boyle**, Attorney/Mediator, Seattle, WA, www.gingerboyle.com

"*The Collaborative Divorce Advantage* offers clients and therapists alike easy-to-understand, sound, legal alternatives to the high emotional and financial costs of litigated divorce. I will recommend the Child Specialist chapter to every divorcing parent I work with to help them understand how their choice of a Child Specialist can impact their children's well-being for years to come."

— **Nancy Ross**, LCSW, BCD, Co-Author of *Divorce, A Problem to be Solved; Not a Battle to be Fought*, co-creator of the Collaborative Interdisciplinary team concept, Collaborative Divorce Coach, Mediator, Trainer, Psychotherapist & Collaborative Communication Specialist for Trusts & Estates www.bsrcounselingservices.com/biographies

"I strongly recommend that you read this book if you are heading into divorce or helping couples. Coming at the tail end of a tunnel of heartache and failed efforts to reconcile, divorce has the potential to set the stage for both partners to chart a new course. Yet divorce can be draining and acrimonious, with unmitigated loss and emotional suffering. *The Collaborative Divorce Advantage* is unique in calling upon partners to walk through the process with eyes open, defining and living into their higher values, while acquiring the skills needed to stick to those values. Divorcing partners have the opportunity to manage emotional distress and hazardous relationship challenges wisely and skillfully, sparing their wallets and their restructuring family relationships for the future."

— **Charles Swenson**, MD
Expert Trainer/Consultant/Author regarding Dialectical Behavior Therapy and Borderline Personality Disorder, Associate Clinical Professor of Psychiatry, University of Massachusetts Medical School

Avoid A Lifetime of Regret: Make An Informed Decision on How You Choose to Divorce

"Discourage litigation. Persuade your neighbors to compromise whenever you can. Point out to them how the nominal winner is often the real loser - in fees, expenses, and waste of time."
-Abraham Lincoln

When faced with the possibility of divorce, too many people fail to realize they have options. They often are caught up in the emotions and pain from the past to take the necessary pause and reflect on the process, and understand their options.

Having watched family and friends struggle through divorce, and experiencing divorce myself, most people think that a family law court divorce is the only way to end their marriage. Some couples may even stay married longer, afraid that such a combative process may harm their children.

Divorce isn't one size fits all, however, and progressive divorce professionals now realize the benefits of providing different divorce methods that are better suited to divorcing couples. Why? Because *how* you divorce matters.

When contemplating divorce, deciding on the divorce process is critical and will impact your life and your children's lives now and for years to come. The method one chooses for divorce can affect both parties' finances and the well-being of all involved.

The Four Divorce Process Paths

The Litigation Path

The most common divorce path to date remains the litigation path. In the litigation path, each spouse hires a family law attorney, and the divorce is handled in family law court. In essence, you are suing one another. This forces divorcing spouses to form alliances, thereby causing tensions to rise, and the divorce can quickly become contentious. Emotions tend to be strong, and worse, are on display in a public courtroom.

There is often this idea of a "winner" or a "loser." Frequently, however, both parties lose after depleting resources arguing over minor things. In addition, both parties will require legal representation and other professionals to prove their case before a judge. A judge will then ultimately decide how their lives will be crafted going forward.

Even if one is educated on the different divorce paths, sometimes one or both divorcing spouses may still choose a litigated divorce because they remain stuck in the past and feel a need to battle it out in court to seek revenge.

However, many couples may feel pushed towards this path without knowledge of their divorce options. They don't honestly view their former partners as adversaries and want to do what is best for their children. But these other methods have not been presented to them. Too often, people who have gone through divorce trauma learn about alternative options later and regret their litigated divorce.

The Paperwork Path

On the other end of the spectrum is the "just the paperwork" path. On this path, both parties can easily compromise and agree to split marital assets without the aid of a judge. They simply need help from a lawyer or paralegal to draft the paperwork. This path is ideal for non-contentious divorcing spouses that do not have children.

The Collaborative Divorce Path

The kinder, gentler path is that of Collaborative Divorce. This path is frequently the best course for those with children. In addition, its comprehensive approach ensures that all parties—divorcing partners and their children—emerge with the tools they need to craft their new lives. Not only does that mean fairer financial settlements but also co-parenting tools and new methods for communicating.

This book will explore the Collaborative Divorce and Divorce Mediation Paths in more depth and provide information for couples seeking to separate in a healthier way.

Attorney Stu Webb, when detailing his idea of Collaborative Practice in 1990, shared a vision of two parties working together to a mutually beneficial goal. In this original iteration, the lawyers from each side voluntarily agree that they will not represent their clients if the collaborative process fails and the case must go to trial. While this is still a central tenet of Collaborative Practice and Collaborative Law, much has changed.

When first introduced, Collaborative Practice provided attorneys with an alternative dispute resolution method. For those tired of litigation and worried about the effects of contentious court battles, the timing was perfect. Since 1990, attorneys, financial professionals, and mental health professionals have worked hard to establish Collaborative Practice as a valid, useful method for approaching legal problems. To date, Collaborative Practice has been especially beneficial as a divorce method.

Collaborative Divorce has emerged as a way for divorcing couples to work together to separate. Rather than requiring two litigating attorneys who present their sides to a judge, the collaborative method relies on a team of professionals and a commitment to transparency. The goal of the collaborative team is to shepherd former partners through the divorce process while helping them construct the agreements they need to craft their separate lives post-divorce. The team makeup is dependent on the needs of the parties, ensuring that each divorce and relationship is treated as a unique entity.

To adhere to these principles and to bring value to the process, Collaborative Divorce professionals must undergo training in collaborative practice. Since it is a relatively new practice, it is often necessary for former litigators to learn new methods for handling disputes and how best to work together with other professionals. Financial neutrals, divorce coaches, and child specialists must learn how to work with both parties to ensure that everyone's needs are being met and that the divorcing parties have the tools and resources they require to transition safely.

Attorneys trained in Collaborative Practice understand the need to present their potential clients with all possible divorce options. They explain the benefits and drawbacks and assist clients in choosing an option.

When a Collaborative Divorce seems the best fit, it is necessary to get both parties on board. If both sides agree to a Collaborative Divorce; the focus shifts to encouraging transparency, developing a team, and working together to determine the needs and interests of both parties.

At its most basic, the collaborative team consists of two collaboratively trained attorneys and their clients. A financial neutral, the Certified Divorce Financial Analyst (CDFA™), is often added to help equitably distribute the marital assets and to assist in determining child support and alimony. A Divorce Coach is frequently added to help the divorcing spouses navigate through the process. In some cases, two Divorce Coaches are used, one for each partner and the financial neutral is tasked with running the meetings. For cases that involve children, it is advised that a Collaborative Child Specialist (CS) is part of the team. The CS helps bring the voice and concerns of the children to the table.

The different issues divorcing couples face, such as the division of marital assets, are generally handled in full team meetings, as are the drafting of documents. Smaller meetings may be held to prepare team members to deal with issues and to help move the process along. Throughout, transparency and openness help the process move forward without the push and pull often seen in litigated cases.

In this book, you'll have the opportunity to learn more about these roles from practicing professionals.

The Collaborative Law Attorney

Authored by a practicing collaborative divorce lawyer, chapter one will explain how working together through divorce can better serve all involved parties and how redefining what a successful divorce is can positively impact the process. Kevin J. Chroman, Esq., details the pitfalls of litigation and how collaborative divorce or divorce mediation can better serve the needs of separating couples.

The Certified Divorce Financial Analyst (CDFA™)

The role of the CDFA™ and the importance of financial planning is explained in chapters three and four.

In chapter three, Kevin R. Worthley, CFP®, CDFA™, shows how a financial planner can help spouses avoid costly financial mistakes during the divorce process.

In chapter four, William M. Morris, CDFA™, covers how creative solutions can help divorcing spouses save money even when they're separating their assets.

The Collaborative Child Specialist (CS)

Chapter five highlights the unique position of the Collaborative Child Specialist in protecting children throughout a divorce. Ria Severance, LMFT, focuses on how the CS can help children avoid the negative fall-out following a divorce and details what divorcing spouses can do for their children right now.

The Divorce Coach

Dominique Walmsley, MA, LMHC, authored chapter six which focuses on the role of the Divorce Coach in the collaborative process. Dominique highlights how those going through the divorce process must learn to manage the conflict and emotional turmoil that comes with divorce.

Together, these team members help participants find common ground and focus on their best interests so that their agreements are crafted with those goals in mind. Whereas courtroom battles frequently focus on "getting more," Collaborative Divorce agreements focus on meeting the needs of everyone involved and providing mutually beneficial agreements and parenting plans.

Will Collaborative Divorce Work for Me?

Divorce can be traumatic. Any efforts to minimize the pain can be helpful. However, Collaborative Divorce isn't for everyone. To determine whether a Collaborative Divorce is appropriate, consider the advantages and disadvantages.

Advantages

A Collaborative Divorce:

- Allows participants to have a voice in the process and the agreements.
- Is open and transparent.
- Can be quicker or slower depending on the needs of the participants.
- May be more affordable than a traditionally litigated divorce.
- Creates agreements that, thanks to the input of the participants, tend to be more equitable and keep the best interest of all involved in mind.
- Results in agreements which participants are more likely to abide by since they had a hand in crafting them.
- Focuses on everyone's best interests.
- Keeps the children front and center.
- Supports participants through the process.
- May be less expensive in the long run.
- Keeps an eye on the future by anticipating needs.
- Helps transition partners into co-parents.

Disadvantages

A Collaborative Divorce:

- Requires two willing participants committed to the process.
- Typically, more expensive than mediation related to a multi-professional team. But less expensive than a drawn-out litigation process.
- May not be appropriate for divorces that involve substance abuse, mental health problems, or domestic violence.
- Requires new lawyers if the collaborative process breaks down.

No relationship is the same. While these are generalized advantages and disadvantages, speaking to a trained collaborative professional can provide you with a clearer picture as to how a Collaborative Divorce may work in your situation.

Ready to Learn More?

If you'd like to learn more about the Collaborative Divorce process and speak to a professional, the authors of this book have shared their contact information. You can also visit *www.collaborativepractice.com/public/search-professionals. aspx* to locate a Collaborative Divorce professional in your area.

The Divorce Mediation Path

Another alternative to a traditional litigated divorce, Divorce Mediation focuses on the same benefits as Collaborative Divorce but arrives at them through different methods.

In Divorce Mediation, a separating couple meets with a trained mediator to amicably dissolve their marriage and create agreements. The clients lead the process and with the aid of a mediator craft agreements that work well for both parties. A mediator is a neutral individual who does not offer advice, though they do aid with brainstorming and help divorcing parties move forward through the divorce process.

For some divorces, all that is necessary is a Divorce Mediator. Other divorces may benefit from the use of a mediation team that includes specialists to help the parties best formulate agreements that will serve them well in the future. Attorney mediators, parenting coaches or mediators, accountant mediators, or financial counselors may all be useful members of the team. It is truly up to the divorcing couple to determine the makeup of their team and to decide what input they need to end their marriage amicably.

The Divorce Mediator

In Chapter two, John C. Hoelle, J.D., and Peter M. Fabish, J.D., MA, focus on the benefits of Conscious Divorce Mediation. They detail the effects of conflict on the health and wellbeing of children and parents and present how Conscious Divorce Mediation works to create a less-stressful environment for divorcing couples to separate amicably.

Will Divorce Mediation Work for Me?

Mediation is often recommended for couples who have maintained good communication despite their desire to divorce. The following advantages and disadvantages can help you make a preliminary decision about whether Divorce Mediation may be a good option for you.

Advantages

Divorce Mediation:

- Is less expensive than traditional divorce.

- Has a smaller team than a Collaborative Divorce.

- Is generally quicker than a litigated divorce.

- Usually, ends in settlement.

- Is confidential; whereas the court records of a litigated divorce are public records, the mediation sessions are not.

- Is led by the participants.

- Can improve communication.

Disadvantages

Divorce Mediation:

- Is only appropriate if both parties are ready to divorce.

- May not be suitable for divorces where domestic violence, substance abuse, or mental health problems are an issue.

- Requires good communication from both parties.

Ready to Learn More?

If you're interested in learning more about whether Divorce Mediation is the best choice for your divorce, contact a local Divorce Mediator. You can search for someone in your area at *www.mediate.com*. If you live in the metro Denver / Boulder Colorado area, check out the contact details for co-authors John Hoelle and Peter Fabish in chapter two.

Comparing Collaborative Divorce and Divorce Mediation

Both Collaborative Divorce and Divorce Mediation provide separating couples with options outside of the traditional litigation route. While they may seem similar in nature, some important differences should be kept in mind when selecting a divorce method.

Divorce Mediation, at its most basic, requires only a neutral mediator who may or may not be an attorney. Collaborative Divorce requires at least two lawyers trained in Collaborative Practice. These lawyers represent their clients and are not neutral, though they are working towards resolution.

Both options allow for additional team members as needed and take less time than a litigated divorce. Divorce Mediation is generally quicker than Collaborative Divorce, however, especially if fewer professionals are involved in the process.

Both Collaborative Divorce and Divorce Mediation aim to reduce contentiousness and create space for brainstorming and resolution. Both are appropriate for divorcing couples who can communicate despite the divorce.

Collaborative Divorce and Divorce Mediation provide valid alternatives to the battle scenes of the courtroom. The chapters that follow will serve to distinguish the two processes further.

Note on Hiring a Divorce Professional

When hiring any divorce professional, it is important that you feel comfortable speaking with them. All divorce professionals should be upfront and open with you. During your consultation with a collaborative professional or a mediator, feel free to ask about other professionals they have worked with as well as the training they have taken and similar cases they've had.

If you already have a lawyer, they may be able to provide you with a list of other collaboratively trained professionals with whom they've worked and who they believe may be a good fit for your team. Meet with these individuals yourself and discuss your situation before moving forward.

Remember, a divorce professional referral from a colleague, friend or family member may or may not be your best option. Just because they had a great experience with the professional does not mean you will also, nor does it guarantee the divorce professional is ethical or has your family's best interest in mind. Take the time to vet these referrals appropriately.

Lastly, please note that this book is not intended to be construed as legal advice and that you should always seek the opinion of a professional to gain insight into your case.

Renee Harrison
Editor-in-Chief, Author, Marketer & Publisher
www.mogulymedia.com
Divorce Reform Advocate
www.divorcebuddy.co

SECTION 1: STAY OUT OF COURT

CHAPTER ONE

How to Avoid the Prisoner's Dilemma in Your Divorce

by Kevin J. Chroman, Esq.

*"The secret of change is to focus all of your
energy not on fighting the old,
but on building the new."*
-Socrates

The Prisoner's Dilemma. You've seen the scenario unfold dozens of times in film or on a TV crime series. Two criminal suspects are arrested and immediately separated with no means of communicating. The prosecution, lacking enough evidence to convict the pair, attempts to get confessions out of the alleged criminals by convincing them to betray each other, promising to charge them on a lesser charge if they testify against each other.

The two suspects have two options: 1) Identify the other party as "not guilty"; 2) Identify the other party as "guilty." Albert W. Tucker formalized the concept in game theory characterizing the potential scenarios:

Scenario 1: If Prisoner A and Prisoner B betray each other, they'll each serve two years in prison.

Scenario 2: If Prisoner A betrays Prisoner B (and Prisoner B keeps hush), Prisoner A is set free, while Prisoner B is sentenced to 3 years in prison (or vice versa).

Scenario 3: If both prisoners remain silent, the prosecution won't have enough evidence to charge either of them with the more severe charge. Both will only serve a year in prison.

Kevin Chroman, Esq., professor of law at Loyola Law School and a Collaborative Divorce practitioner, explains how this classic game theory applies to family law and what we can learn from it to approach divorce in a less adversarial manner.

Jeremy Kossen: Before we dive into the "prisoner's dilemma," how it applies to family law, and why collaborative law is a much better alternative, can you share what the basis was for your decision to switch from family law litigation to collaborative law? Was it just being exposed to Collaborative Divorce, or was there a defining moment in litigation where you told yourself, "This is not the way to do this."

Kevin Chroman, Esq.: I remember having one case where I had a client who was not married. The father had two or three children from two separate women, one of which was my client's son. He happened to have money not from his income, but from his family. He could provide well and live in exclusive areas of Los Angeles, like Newport Beach or Beverly Hills. He was very spiteful towards the mother of the child, and not only would he not see his son, he wouldn't make any efforts to see him either.

It was very clear to me that this child benefited greatly from being with his mother more than his father. We got a psychological evaluation on the father, and based on the battery of tests, everything the mother said about him—all the negative psychological issues she accused him of —came out as true. He tested positive, so to speak, for all her accusations.

However, the psychologist who analyzed the test seemed to favor men and decided that the son should primarily be with the father, despite the father's behavior and testing. And the mother, who had a modest earning job would need to move closer to the upscale neighborhood of Newport Beach if she wanted more time with her son. This living arrangement was financially oppressive to the mother. She could not afford to move, and she was not readily employable.

In the end, the mother had to decide between her job and her child. Essentially, she was left with no decision as she could not afford the neighborhood near the father's home. Ironically, the father could not afford to live there either, except for the financial support of his grandparents. To try and object to the findings of this court expert, we would have had to throw more money at another expert. Our client did not have the money, and we were unable to get more money from the father because his grandparents were his source of income. This case was one of the defining moments where it just felt like this indeed was justice gone awry. It had more to do with this evaluator than anybody else. The mother didn't have as much money as the father to object to the findings and hire a new expert. Money and bias, not justice, won the day. And, within collaborative law, it is precisely those types of power imbalances we try to be aware of and equalize.

The Prisoner's Dilemma & Family Law

Jeremy: How does the "prisoner's dilemma" apply to family law?

Kevin: The classic concept of the "prisoner's dilemma" illustrates why two completely "rational" individuals might not cooperate, even if it appears that it is in their best interests to do so. This same scenario commonly plays out in family law litigation when spouses separate into their "opposing corners" by initiating a litigious divorce from the outset. Often, one or both parties "breaks their silence" by attacking the opposing party.

Imagine what the outcome would be if each person weren't first separated. That first step of separating them creates an environment of distrust, as they don't know what the other person is planning to do. Therefore, they fear the worst and hedge their bets, so to speak, by implicating the other person. This separation all but assures them of avoiding the "maximum sentence." However, since they are both likely to take this approach, it assures them of serving time. Had they had an opportunity to cooperate, they could have each gone free, virtually. That's the whole essence of it.

Collaborative family law is different from family law litigation because it is built on the premise that beginning from a place of transparency and trust will lead to a better outcome, both financially and emotionally, than when beginning from a position of opposition. Imagine if the prisoners had a chance to talk about their options with one another first. Everyone would agree that the opportunity to speak with one another would make it much easier for each to receive an outcome they wanted.

Jeremy: In divorce, how common do you think outright false accusations are versus gross exaggerations?

Kevin: That's a good question. Both happen. I've heard horror stories from my colleagues that ever since the courts dismissed the approach of fathers receiving every other weekend visitations and approached each case with the presumption that moms and dads are to obtain 50/50 custody, domestic violence actions have significantly increased. Domestic violence is a basis to award limited custody to the offending party. Therefore, it is used as a weapon for a parent to achieve the goal of being awarded additional custody.

On several occasions, I've heard stories where the person charged with domestic violence did not engage in that behavior at all, yet they were accused of it and had to go several months without seeing their children. Minors' counsel and therapists often need to get involved—only to find out that that the accuser was just lying all along to try to get the best custody orders.

There are stories like that, but I would say the more common issue is when parties come out with "guns blazing" and write declarations regarding the other parent to attempt to get more custody or more money. The parent, with the assistance of counsel, may stretch the truth about the other parent to place themselves in the best position to benefit. Maybe they are not outright lies, but they are an over-magnification of the person's negative traits to lead the court to believe that this is all he or she is.

If we apply the prisoner's dilemma to this issue, we can see the parents may feel as if they have nothing to lose since they are already at 50/50 custody. Therefore, the thinking goes, if I can paint a bleak enough picture of the other parent, I can only improve my chances of getting more custody. Often, this serves little more than to eradicate any goodwill that may have remained in the relationship while creating a more hostile relationship between the parents.

> *"Family law can be an art, and part of the art is depicting your client in the best light, which often includes painting the other person in their worst light."*

Family law can be an art, and part of the art is depicting your client in the best light. Too often this includes painting the other person in their worst light. Everyone has some negative traits, and the goal is to magnify those qualities for the court so they only see the negative traits of the other parent. The reality is that everybody has some bad days, but mostly we have good days. And we have a lot of days in between that are just neutral.

Jeremy: Do you think judges are good at deciphering lies or an attorney's over-magnification of negative portrayals of the other spouse?

Kevin: I certainly give our judges a lot of credit. I think they do a good job of deciphering exaggerations. Some of the best judges approach the dynamic I described earlier with an attitude of: "You were able to co-parent for your entire marriage, which has been 10 to 15 years. It's hard for me to believe that now that you're getting divorced the other person is so evil and wicked they are incapable of co-parenting with you, and vice versa. I'm going to work on the assumption that you both are capable of working together, and if something material arises, you can let me know, but I'm not going to make any judgments based on the mudslinging that has occurred." I've heard a few judges say this sort of thing, and I have a lot of respect for them and that initial approach.

Unless it rises to the level of something truly material—if your spouse has abandoned your child or placed them in danger—then that's something else that requires a ruling by a judge. But if you just raised your voice or were late, or you've been mean and hurtful, that doesn't rise to the level of judges typically making orders. Nonetheless, as an attorney, that's what you want to put forth. So, if any of this behavior comes up again, you can point to it and say, "As we stated in our original declaration, your honor, the father has tendencies of doing this only to spite the mother. He has tendencies of being late and changes plans at the very last minute."

Attorneys make those points because they want to put their clients in the best position if something happens in the future. It is the Prisoner's Dilemma. I want to get my negative depiction of the other side out there in anticipation of A) something happening in the future and B) how would it look if we said, "This person's a great guy." In the meantime, the judge reads something stating, "The wife is an awful woman who never gives the husband or the kids a moment of peace." You want to hedge your bets against that at the very least.

The Prisoner's Dilemma, in a way, is about betting. It's how you bet, and how you hedge your bets. Lest the other person writes something negative about us, we should do the same so that at the very least the judge shrugs his or her shoulders and says, "Okay, you both have complaints against each other, I'm going to take the middle road." If it appears lopsided, then your client might turn to you and say, "I have negative things to say about that person. You told me not to. You said we should take the high road. But look at all the scathing things they wrote about me. I'm afraid that's going to influence the judge."

Jeremy: How does this dynamic affect co-parenting?

Kevin: Attorneys may magnify and exacerbate the negative traits in the other spouse for all these strategic purposes. Irrespective of whether the judge takes that into account when making their orders, it does affect the ability of the parent to co-parent. It hurts and defeats both parent's capacity for healthy co-parenting.

It's one thing to have an argument behind closed doors and air your personal opinions about each other. It's another thing when you've now shared it with a third party, your attorney, and in open court. Once a person has put it on paper, in print, and submitted it to a court, there's something formal and official about it. You can't take it back, and it often erodes the co-parenting relationship even more. Starting out with guns blazing and throwing mud makes it difficult for a parent to recover from words so clearly intended to harm, and hurt. Whoever wrote "sticks and stones can break my bones, but words will never hurt me," clearly was never the subject of a declaration written by a skilled family law attorney.

Litigation Is Chess, Collaborative Law Is a Puzzle

Jeremy: How does collaborative law differ from litigation?

Kevin: Litigation becomes a chess game—how do we outmaneuver the other person? Collaborative law, on the other hand, is more of a puzzle to try to achieve satisfaction for everybody. To create a picture where all the pieces can come together. In litigation, like chess, someone must win and someone must lose. The "opponent" is pushed into a corner and must be checkmated until they concede to your position.

There are cases where people behave badly, and they deserve to be countered in front of the judge. For example, it may be appropriate when people are misbehaving regarding their children, or failing to provide complete information regarding assets and debts. Some cases have those elements. However, most cases can achieve resolution without that level of gamesmanship.

Jeremy: That's a great analogy. It's either a chess game or putting the pieces of a puzzle together. They're very distinct strategies with very different outcomes.

Kevin: One strategy is about cooperating to create an agreement together, where you both embrace the puzzle and the outcome. It's made up of a lot of fractured pieces, but we can put those pieces together to create a structure which both parties can agree upon. Litigation is much more like chess. How can I position everything? When it comes to litigation, it's not only the substantive things such as declarations that paint somebody in a poor light.

For example, sometimes people receive requests for discovery immediately before the holidays. Or right before the holidays, people get ex parte notice to appear in court the following day. There are procedural games that seasoned attorneys may play that are harmful to the parental relationship and deteriorates that relationship even more because it shows a deep and profound disrespect for the other person and their time.

> *"If your goal is to upset your ex-spouse and beat them into submission, collaborative law is not for you. If your goal is to go through this process in the most reasonable way, under tough circumstances, collaborative divorce is for you."*

Many different levers can be pushed to upset the other person in a divorce case. If your goal is to upset your ex-spouse and force them to submit to your perspective, collaborative law is not for you. If your goal is to go through this process in the most reasonable way under tough circumstances, collaborative divorce is for you.

Nobody says you should be best friends, but nobody says you have to be lifelong enemies, either. If your goal is to effectively co-parent your children and provide them the best opportunity to be healthy young men and women, your aim is to have a working relationship with your ex-spouse. You can accomplish this through a resolution-oriented process through collaborative divorce law.

Redefining Divorce "Success" Metrics

Jeremy: It seems the "success" metrics that we base divorce on aren't very good. In the context of traditional divorce litigation, there's an accepted success metric of "who can get the most."

"I want to get the most spousal and child support." Or, "I deserve the most time with the kids." Those are not metrics that are necessarily beneficial to anybody. These are the kind of metrics that pump up the amount of money it's going to cost to go through the divorce process and takes a parent away from a child.

However, if we embrace the collaborative approach and define success as not wasting a bunch of money, ensuring our kids are as healthy and happy as possible, and creating a reasonable co-parenting relationship, then we're going to take a much different approach to our divorce, and everyone wins.

We're working with the wrong outcomes.

Kevin: Precisely. I think it's a matter of stating your goals and being clear about those goals. I think most people want a "fair" settlement. Of course, fairness is subjective. That is one of the first things we ask a client to define for us in a case while informing them that the other parent's idea of fairness may differ.

Ultimately, if you want to be on the other side of this process and have a civil relationship with the other parent, have a good relationship with your kids, shield the kids from unnecessary negative feelings, and save money, then the collaborative process is for you. If you want to be in control of the expenses in the case, collaborative divorce provides that. And, if you want an arena to constructively express your feelings and concerns with the assistance of mental health professionals who are proficient in that area, collaborative law provides that as well.

> *"If you want to be on the other side of this process and have a civil relationship with the other parent, have a good relationship with your kids, shield the kids from unnecessary negative feelings, and save money, then the collaborative process is for you."*

However, if you want to make a personal statement of the anger and animosity you have towards your spouse, in a public forum and spend a lot of money to make sure that your points are heard, then you could do that in a litigated divorce. But in the end, I don't think that there's a high satisfaction level for that, especially in the long term.

In my opinion, most cases would greatly benefit from beginning in a resolution-oriented process, such as a collaborative process or mediation. The benefit would be felt financially, as well as in the quality of the relationships post-divorce. One can always escalate towards litigation, however, once litigation starts, it becomes harder to de-escalate.

To recap, one should determine if their case is an extreme case, which requires immediate or material intervention by a court. If the case does not fall into that category, then perhaps the next question should be, "What process allows me to address my issues in a manner that best considers my finances, my relationship with my kids and my ex-spouse, and my psychological peace of mind?"

Litigation Is a Game of Conflict

Kevin: Litigation attorneys have many skills, and their perceived purpose is to know how to fight for you and defend you against attacks. As I referenced earlier, sometimes the best defense is a good offense. Therein starts the cycle. Instead of tempering your emotions and turning to their clients and saying, "Okay, how could we resolve these things? I understand your feelings." Instead, an attorney may run with a client's charged feelings. Some would argue that this occurs more often when there's a lot of money in the case. When you have two people who don't like each other, and then you have two attorneys who are taught not to trust their opposing counsel until proven otherwise, you have a dilemma. Or, more accurately, you have a double prisoner's dilemma.

Think about it...now you have four people, each with their different personalities, skin in the game, some level of anxiety, and some level of animosity. If any one of those four people is having a bad day, all four of them have a bad day. You have four participants: two attorneys who are taught to fight and the two parties who initially want to fight because they don't know any better. For everything to settle down and get resolved, all four of those people need to lay down their arms. All four of them need to agree to refrain from pointing a finger of blame at the other. All four need to make the wise choice made in the Prisoner's Dilemma.

If you think about divorce as a game, what happens when you're not in control of your own game? If you're playing chess with somebody, you can say, "You know what? Let's call it a tie." But in litigation, there are two other people who are saying, "You can't do that, and we're going to start moving the pieces around to make sure that this is not going to be a tie." Suddenly, it's not your game. You're not in control of your own game.

In collaborative law, both parties have control over the process. They identify what the agenda is going to be during a meeting. There's a buy-in of what goes into the agenda. There's complete transparency about how the team will approach that agenda and the information they're going to need. There's no second guessing. There's nothing hidden. Self-determination is a paramount component of collaborative law.

Jeremy: Most states require a six-month cooling off period before formally beginning the divorce. Does this help?

Kevin: Divorce is an intensely psychological event, and that's part of the reason you can't get divorced for six months. The court wants you to have a cooling off period. Unfortunately, during those six months, much of this litigation is initiated. Motions can be filed in month two or three that aren't heard until month seven or eight. The groundwork of opposition is laid during the first couple of months and by month 7 or 8, it's often too late to reverse course. You've already planted the seeds that are going to be bearing fruit (albeit unhealthy fruit) three, four, five months down the road.

> *"There are various studies which show that a person's psychology during a divorce is tantamount to one who has experienced the loss of a loved one or similar significant trauma."*

People are usually so angry and fearful in the first months of their separation that they're usually not thinking straight. There are various studies which show that a person's psychology during a divorce is tantamount to one who has experienced the loss of a loved one or similar significant trauma. And, it is during this very emotionally and psychologically charged time that they are required to make critical decisions about their future, as well as the way their divorce is handled. If they elect to pursue litigation, they may not be aware of how difficult and costly it may become to ultimately resolve the case.

Financial Advantages of Collaborative Law Divorce

Kevin: I run a clinic at the Loyola Law School where we perform collaborative divorces. We get a team together, including a mediator, and we give free services. We have two attorneys, coaches, and a financial neutral. Most of the folks we help are of modest means, but they have very real issues, and we resolve them. We resolve them in six hours. Sometimes it takes two sessions, 12 hours. Other times they come back to go over some things just with the mediator alone, so let's say 15 hours in those cases. Somewhere between six to fifteen hours, their cases get resolved, though usually, it's closer to six hours.

Within the clinic, we experience some of the very same issues that are experienced by wealthy people, the two biggest being custody and the family residence. Often. it's either about when dad or mom should be with the kids and ensuring everyone has adequate time with the children, or how we will deal with the family residence when that is the primary residence for the children and has significant equity. These issues are addressed with little cost, little time, and less animosity within the collaborative clinic.

Then when the same issues arise, and a party happens to be a baseball player or doctor, they can't seem to engage in a resolution-oriented approach until the very end of the case—after a tremendous amount of money has been spent. It makes me wonder why these same issues, with a lot more zeroes after the person's income and assets, cannot get resolved earlier. Could those same problems have been addressed in a process that is typically faster, calmer, and less expensive?

In high net-worth cases, they often cannot seem to come to an agreement early. Is the attorney turning to them and saying, "Look, this is in the realm of fairness. You could spend $100,000 more or you could just settle it like this..." Or, "All right, it's 10 to 15% less parenting time than you wanted. You could always come back in a couple of years and see how things are going." Or, is the litigating attorney saying: "Let's fight this. How dare they offer you 10% less time or money than you wanted!" Moreover, if a client is being unreasonable, are they keeping them in check? Or, are they perpetuating their unreasonable positions?

Jeremy: Yes, that's an important point as well. A litigator may have a financial incentive to continue litigating. But in collaborative divorce, do you have those same built-in financial incentives to prolong it?

Kevin: I want to take a moment to clarify. My focus is more on the process and less on attaching motives to attorneys within a process. I know many litigating attorneys, indeed most, who are ethical beyond reproach. However, because litigation attorneys can be the "drivers" of the litigation process, it leaves them open to criticism that perhaps a case was not settled sooner due to personal interests. The attorney doesn't have the same influence within the collaborative model as they may have within litigation. By that I mean, a collaborative case has the client driving the process, not the attorney. As attorneys, we are often asked to be hand-holders, as well as review various financial documents and other functions. And though we develop many of those skills, there is a limit on those roles. In fact, within the collaborative process, you have coaches and financial experts involved, which reduces the amount of "hats" an attorney is often asked to wear. For example, if there is an issue which has an intensely emotional or psychological component and may function to limit one's openness to compromise, those issues are explored by mental health professionals who have degrees within that field.

As a collaborative attorney, I am trained to listen and ask questions to get to the interests of clients. However, the coaches have been trained for years to draw out what's going on behind the scenes emotionally and psychologically and coach that person on presenting his or her ideas. Their capacity to do so creates a financial benefit to the client as it is more efficient for the individual and the process for ideas and concerns to be expressed constructively.

Similarly, the financial expert, who is neutral, can provide tremendous guidance and resources to the financial issues of a case. Again, this saves money for a client by having issues presented by a neutral professional, rather than attorneys arguing over different approaches to a financial issue.

The division of labor ultimately saves both clients money while providing the best information from the most appropriate professional resource. Moreover, the attorney's hourly rate is often the highest of the professionals. Therefore, the client benefits from the best-suited professional addressing their need, often at a lower rate than the one who is less well suited to address that issue.

A collaborative attorney will earn money on a case, however, their capacity to increase the cost of a case or discourage compromise is far more limited than a litigation model. They cannot file oppositional documents with the court or engage in behavior that directly results in incurring fees. If they do behave in that manner, the team will let them know. And, though I do not believe most litigators function from that perspective, the potential and opportunity for that behavior exists to a far greater degree within the litigation model as compared to the collaborative model.

To simplify, a lot of attorneys in litigation enjoy a good fight, and a lot of collaborative attorneys enjoy a good resolution. That's just how they're wired. And, in my experience, fighting typically costs more than resolving.

Jeremy: That's a good point. Their internal success metrics are different too, like the fight. If you're a litigator, you're motivated by the fight. That's part of the "fun." Whereas collaboration, its success metric is, "Did we come to an amicable resolution?"

Kevin: That's right. It's that win/lose mentality, which fighters often have, versus a win/win mentality associated with those who like to find compromise and a middle ground.

Shifting Gears: Switching Between Litigation and Collaboration

Jeremy: Can you discuss the pros and cons and why it's beneficial to start off in the collaborative process? And if you've already gone down the path of litigation, how do you extricate yourself and do a reset toward a more collaborative process?

Kevin: When you begin the collaborative process, you agree to approach the issues with honesty and goodwill towards one another and the process. If for some reason, the parties are unable to maintain the transparency and civility the process requires, they can always elect to litigate the issues. But they must do so with the assistance of new counsel. Shifting the divorce into litigation means they must incur the additional expense of hiring someone new and getting them acquainted with the issues of the case. That cost functions as a deterrent. However, the cost is not prohibitive.

Starting off in collaborative, you always have the option of going to a different process. However, if you elect to litigate first, it's difficult, and highly unlikely, that the case can then become a collaborative case. This is true primarily because both parties would have to agree on the collaborative process. Not only would you have to fire your attorney, but your spouse would have to fire their attorney, and everybody would have to get new counsel and a team. The likelihood of wanting to pay for collaborative divorce professionals to get up to speed on what's been going on in your case is slim.

It becomes very impractical to switch from litigation to collaborative law. It's not impossible, but it's not likely. However, while people are in litigation, they can insist on using a mediator and go to mediation as often as they like if they feel that that's a better way of dealing with things. It would be tough for both parties who are in litigation to mutually agree to mediation or embark on collaborative law. If they're willing to agree to go to a collaborative process, they're probably willing to agree to resolve some of their issues at that point, and mediation would be the more likely process.

Parents & Post-Litigation Regret

Jeremy: How did we get in the situation where litigation is the default position?

Kevin: I think the reasons mediation and collaborative law are not the default first approaches to the divorce process are due to our culture, money, and recent changes within the law. Each is a big factor in all of this.

Prior to mediation and collaborative law coming into to the legal picture, the only way to be assured that your divorce was being completed within the parameters of the law was to hire attorneys to address your case through the litigation process. There was virtually no other viable option. Moreover, there was inequality within the approach towards custody and finances. Men were not given equal rights regarding custody, and women were not provided equal rights in the workplace. Men saw their kids less and were responsible for financial support. Women had more time with the kids, but they had less opportunity for self-support. Those issues are a breeding ground for fighting. And, from that model, a cultural standard was created. Movies, TV shows, books, were all generated which romanticized the divorce. I use the term "romanticize" loosely, as many of the depictions are rather horrific. Nonetheless, those media reflected what people believed was common within the process—fighting. And, that is what generations perceived as the "right" approach to divorce. Divorce and fighting were equated.

I believe these next generations will increasingly gravitate towards resolution-oriented models of divorce. After all, this next generation has the benefit of reflection upon their parents' divorce, or their friend's parents, and conclude that they would never want that for themselves nor their children. There are still plenty who believe divorce must be a battle, and its battle cry is "I'll see you in court." However, I believe this generation is far more educated and informed. Moreover, facts which speak of equality, such as custody becoming 50/50, men and women beginning to achieve parity in incomes, and divorce becoming less stigmatized, reduce the amount of animosity. Simply put, people are beginning to recognize that there is less to fight about since they are being treated as equals under the law and in the workplace. And, if that is true, protracted litigation and the attendant costs and fees simply are an unreasonable or unnecessary expense for the average divorcing couple.

Jeremy: Post-divorce, if given the opportunity for a "do-over," do you think most parents would choose to do things differently?

Kevin: I honestly believe if you polled people who went through a litigated divorce and asked them, "If you had to do it all over again, how would you do it?" I think the clear majority would say, "I would have tried to figure out a way to sit down with my ex to hammer things out. Because either somewhere in the beginning or somewhere in the middle, everything got intense and awful. There was a lot of money spent and accusations made. For every accusation made, money gets spent on an expert."

> *"For every accusation made, money gets spent on an expert."*

Most couples do not have truly bad actors. Maybe they want a little bit of a break from the other spouse on marital or child-rearing issues that are important to them. For example, maybe mom prefers to be with the kids a little bit more and feels that she's more adept at that. Maybe dad wants a little break on financial support if he's earning more money. Nothing terrible. Nothing outrageous. Nothing that a few conversations shouldn't be able to address. I think if you ask those people what they wish they had done differently they'd say, "Yes. I would have wanted to start it differently. I would have wanted an attorney who was more in tune with my needs, who started off by speaking towards our issues, and who was cooperative with the other attorney."

> *The honest answer after someone had experienced the divorce litigation process is often: "I wish we chose a process that allowed us to figure things out without all the money and animosity that ensued."*

Jeremy: Thanks, Kevin. Your experiences and insights in this chapter are impactful; I hope it encourages divorcing couples to pursue the collaborative divorce path.

❖

If you live in the greater Los Angeles area and interested in learning more about collaborative law divorce, contact Kevin via email:

ChromanMediation@gmail.com

Key Takeaways

- ✓ Collaborative divorce focuses on common goals and negotiation, helping to avoid the prisoner's dilemma.

- ✓ Focus on where you want to be at the end of the divorce process. "I am who I am today because of the choices I made yesterday." – Eleanor Roosevelt

- ✓ Collaborative divorce includes a team of professionals to ensure everyone's needs are being met.

- ✓ Because of the separation of roles on a collaborative divorce team, collaborative divorce is often less expensive than a litigated divorce.

- ✓ Many families who have gone through a litigative divorce wish they had had more collaborative tools to assist them through the divorce process. Before selecting a divorce process, identify your needs and then choose a process that will help you meet those needs.

- ✓ Once you decide to litigate your divorce, it's exceedingly difficult to turn the tide and take a collaborative approach, however, those who begin with a collaborative approach can always turn to litigation if necessary.

ABOUT KEVIN J. CHROMAN, ESQ

Kevin J. Chroman, Esq. came to be a strong proponent of collaborative law and mediation quite naturally as he believes that people in conflict typically possess the tools to resolve their conflict. This belief has been reinforced through his experiences with litigation. Divorce is an emotional and psychological event, as well as a legal event with financial consequences. Kevin finds mediation and collaborative law are a safe, cost-saving, and smart alternative to litigation for those who place a value on a cooperative environment, a peaceful resolution for themselves and their family members, and building a healthy future.

Kevin is a Loyola Law School graduate (2000) and presently runs a Collaborative Mediation Clinic at Loyola Law School where he is an adjunct professor. He is a UC Berkeley graduate with a Master's degree in English Literature from DePaul University. Kevin is a Family Law practitioner whose practice focuses exclusively on Collaborative Law and Mediation. Presently, he is on the Board of Los Angeles Collaborative Family Law Association (LACFLA), as well as the statewide Collaborative organization CP Cal (Collaborative Practice California), where he assists in promoting collaborative practice.

BUSINESS NAME: Law and Mediation Office of Kevin J. Chroman
WEBSITE: www.collablawyer.com
EMAIL: ChromanMediation@gmail.com
PHONE: 818-528-7755
LOCATION: Sherman Oaks, CA
FACEBOOK: www.facebook.com/chromanlawoffice

CHAPTER TWO

THE CONSCIOUS DIVORCE: SAVE MONEY, PROTECT YOUR KIDS, AND CREATE A BETTER FUTURE

by John C. Hoelle, JD & Peter M. Fabish, JD, MA

"How people treat you is their karma;
how you react is yours."
-Wayne Dyer

The Harvard researcher behind the longest longitudinal study of health and happiness in humans concluded there are two pillars of happiness: "One is love. The other is finding a way of coping with life that does not push love away."[1]

---

[1] *Huffington Post, The 75-Year Study That Found the Secrets to a Fulfilling Life, Pub. August 11, 2013. Viewed at www.huffingtonpost.com/2013/08/11/how-this-harvard-psycholo_n_3727229. html (Jan 9, 2017)*

What does this mean to those of us—half of us, in fact—who end up facing the end of our marriage through divorce?

As it turns out, it means a lot. How you go about transitioning out of marriage can have a lot to do with how much you invite in, or push away, love—and happiness—for the rest of your life.

How You Divorce Matters

While divorce may be the end of a **physical** and **legal** relationship between you and your spouse, the emotional charge of a marriage will for most people continue to exist as a meaningful presence in your mental and emotional life going forward. And if you have children, you are almost never **ending** your relationship with your spouse. You are **transitioning** from one type of relationship (married) to another (co-parenting). As we will see, how you divorce can have a profound impact on your children. It will also have a profound effect on you and your spouse.

The Effects of High Conflict

Research clearly establishes that children are affected, often profoundly, by high conflict between their parents. Effects on children can include depression and anxiety, low academic performance, low self-esteem, drug and alcohol abuse, poor child-parent relationships, and later, poor adult relationships, among other things.[2]

Divorce doesn't improve matters if parents continue to fight. Post-divorce acrimony contributes to the same issues in children as conflict during marriage. Furthermore, the high stress of divorce can cause parents to use conflict as a defense against their painful feelings. Such parents often have great difficulty keeping their children's best interest in mind.[3]

The impact on the children of divorce as a collective is potentially vast. Half of the children born to married parents today will experience the divorce of their parents before they are 18. Of these, another half will witness the dissolution of a second parental marriage. At least one million American children per year are exposed to divorce; and thus, to the potential for the debilitating effects of

---

[2] *Gilmore, Glen A., High-Conflict Separation and Divorce: Options for Consideration, Background Paper presented for Department of Justice, Canada (2004) (updated Jan. 7, 2015) viewed at www. justice.gc.ca/eng/rp-pr/fl-lf/divorce/2004_1/index.html#toc (March 9, 2017) (hereinafter, "High Conflict Separation")*

[3] *Id.*

a high conflict divorce (or the lesser effects of a healthy divorce). [4] It's not hard to see that how we do divorce is going to have a big impact on how healthy our citizenry and our society will be in the coming decades.

Persistent relational conflict is hard on adults, too. Parents who engage in protracted conflict during and after their divorce experience chronic high stress (with its attendant health detriments); lowered work productivity; financial decline; and psycho-social consequences such as loneliness, bitterness, and hopelessness. It usually hurts their relationships with their children too. [5]

And the strain is felt in parents' work productivity and pocketbooks. A 1996 study estimated that American businesses were losing $6 billion per year due to decreased productivity as a result of their employees' marital difficulties. [6] Another study found that in the year following divorce, workers lost an average of over 168 hours of work time—equivalent to a full month of absence. [7] The *average* cost of divorces involving minor children in 2015 (the vast majority of which were conducted with the traditional litigation model) was found to be $21,700; while the average for higher net worth couples was $37,000. [8]

When parents can maintain positive behaviors toward each other and foster positive feelings for one another in their children, outcomes for children have been significantly better. [9] Parents who can empathize with their children's and the other parent's points of view, to be flexible and to remain civil even during conflict help their children to adjust to divorce in a healthy way and save themselves tremendous physical, emotional, and financial strain. [10]

In sum, choosing a way to divorce that minimizes emotional and financial cost and conflict during and after divorce could have a big impact on the future wellbeing of you and your children.

---

[4] *www.children-and-divorce.com/children-divorce-statistics.html (Jan 10, 2017)*

[5] *Brown, J., High Conflict Divorce: Antecedents and Consequences, Behavioral Health (Online), Vol. 1, No. 1 (2014). Available at jghcs.info/index.php/bh/article/download/320/284.*

[6] *Turvey, M. & Olson, D. (2006). Marriage & Family Wellness: Corporate America's Business? (Life Innovations) (available at mfri.ucf.edu/ps/Marriage%20&%20Family%20Wellness_%20 Corporate%20Americas%20Business_%20Surve.pdf (March 9, 2017)*

[7] *Id.*

[8] *Data from Martindale Nolo Research Divorce Study, published at www.family-law.lawyers.com/ divorce/how-much-does-divorce-cost-in-colorado.html (March 9, 2017)*

[9] *High Conflict Separation (2004).*

[10] *Id.*

What Does It Mean to Divorce "Consciously?"

Con-scious (adj): aware of and responding to one's surroundings; awake; having knowledge of; sensitive to.

While the word "conscious" has numerous connotations, its most basic is to be awake and aware. To consciously divorce is to go through divorce deeply grounded in the reality of your situation and the importance of the process to your family's health and well-being.

Consciously divorcing means you approach your divorce knowing that your family will continue, just in a new form. You are aware of your responsibility toward your children and that your actions during your divorce could profoundly affect them, for better or worse. You believe that adhering to a set of values during and after your divorce that is grounded in self-responsibility and love for your children will allow you to look back on how you behaved during this crucial transition without regret in the many years to follow.

By these standards, it is possible to engage in a litigated divorce consciously. However, litigation—especially involving attorneys who do not give priority to these and other "conscious" principles—can make it far more challenging to do so.

What Are the Goals of People Who Participate in Conscious Divorce Mediation?

Many people who participate in Conscious Divorce Mediation are seeking the following:

To Create a Better Life Going Forward

Most people come to the decision to divorce only after they've painfully decided, for whatever reasons, that they and their spouse can't find ways to live happy, fulfilling lives as intimate partners. Unfortunately, many spouses drag the pain of the marriage into their divorce and post-divorce co-parenting. One of your children's highest interests is in having your relationship with your co-parent be civil, functional, respectful, and relatively free of destructive types of conflict. Another is in having both parents be financially solid, with stable households.

Conscious Divorce Mediation is a collaborative process that helps parties to see the bigger picture and to focus on the prize: successful co-parenting, a sound financial structure for the whole family, and a happy life after the transition.

To Minimize the Cost of Their Divorce

Because Conscious Divorce Mediation clients usually do not hire two lawyers but instead hire one neutral attorney-mediator to get them through the process, divorce almost always costs a fraction of what it would take to litigate.

To Minimize Conflict

Mediation with a skillful mediator and willing parties helps people find ways to creatively solve their issues, without resorting to war. They may experience very painful emotions during the process, such as bitterness or betrayal. Nevertheless, they can get through their divorce with solid, rational agreements that give their co-parenting family the best chance to thrive after the divorce. As we've seen, reducing conflict between parents is crucial to protecting children from harm. Moreover, learning to work through conflict can ease tensions for years to come, if and when co-parents disagree on parenting issues.

To Control the Length of the Process

Because the parties are working together with skilled assistance from a mediator, often without evidentiary and procedural requirements imposed in a litigated process, agreements can usually be reached in far less time.

On the other hand, if needed, the parties can take as much time as necessary to work through difficult negotiations, test out parenting plans, or execute on financial transfers before formally "un-tying the knot."

To Create Good Agreements

Nobody likes going to court, especially to be told how to parent by a "stranger in a robe." Court orders handed down after litigation often leave one or both parties unhappy, and there is a high likelihood of non-compliance with the orders, confusion about the orders, and expensive post-decree litigation.

Many people who are getting along reasonably well try to minimize the cost and conflict of divorce by proceeding without professional assistance. They have the idea, often justified, that if lawyers are involved, they'll end up fighting a lot. Unfortunately, most people find that divorce ends up being extremely complicated. Even if they read all the rules and address all the required issues, they end up with poorly crafted or ambiguous agreements and leave out important provisions that a professional would have made sure to address. This can result in parties fighting again later, for no reason.

Parties who consciously divorce often reach good agreements that would be difficult to replicate in a traditional litigated divorce. When people have a sense of authorship over sound legal agreements created with the guidance of an experienced family attorney-mediator, they tend to comply with and follow the clear agreements they made, and they avoid fighting in the future.

The Difference Between Conscious Divorce Mediation and Traditional Divorce

In traditional divorce proceedings, both spouses hire a lawyer. One of them files a petition for divorce and serves the other, who files a response. Their attorneys then negotiate while preparing for trial, doing discovery, filing motions, and otherwise managing the litigation. If the case doesn't settle, each lawyer presents evidence at a hearing and argues on behalf of his or her client to the judge.

Traditional lawyer-advocates, acting in accordance with their training, portray the opposing party as "bad" and their own client as "good." Typically, this makes divorce far more miserable than it needs to be and leaves the parties poorly positioned to be co-parents after the divorce is complete. Traditional lawyer-advocates are also trained—some might say ethically required—to focus on and fight for a very specific, very limited set of interests for their clients, which are defined and constrained by the legal definitions of a client's "rights." Thus, for example, it might seem self-evident to a traditional lawyer-advocate that obtaining the largest possible financial award for their client is the best possible outcome, even if the result is to leave the other spouse—who now must function independently as a co-parent—financially destitute.

In Conscious Divorce Mediation, parties typically do not hire their own lawyers. Through a series of meetings, the parties, with the help of the mediator, reach agreements on all key issues. The mediator's job is to:

- Help the parties navigate the legal process logistically (forms, timing, etc.);

- Neutrally help the parties understand the law, how it applies to their particular situation, and how a judge might look at their case;

- Help the parties discern their most important values, desires, and needs and apply them to the negotiation on how to parent children and divide assets;

- Help the parties keep their eye on their most important values, commitments, and the ultimate prize: a better life post-divorce;

- Propose and explore with the parties creative solutions to sticky areas of conflict; and

- Help the parties arrive at a clear, detailed settlement agreement that will last.

Many people can function as mediators—therapists, social workers, lawyers, or experts in a particular field. Ideally, the mediator has at least received formal training in acting as a mediator. A Conscious Divorce Mediator, however, is a family lawyer trained in mediation and in facilitating Conscious Divorce. Unlike mediators without that background, a Conscious Divorce mediator can educate the parties about the legal landscape of divorce. He or she does not "represent" either party as a lawyer, but guides both parties in reaching a settlement that complies with the law and makes sense for the family.[11] The Conscious Divorce mediator will have tried cases in the couple's jurisdiction, and so can share with them knowledge of how local judges have decided issues similar to those they are facing.

An attorney-mediator will also know common post-divorce pitfalls that are often difficult for people who have not been through a divorce to anticipate and prevent. He or she can help the parties address those issues in their agreements and avoid post-decree conflict.

A Conscious Divorce Mediator may, from time to time, recommend that the parties involve additional professionals in the process to address specific issues. Additional possible team members or consultants may include:

- A divorce financial analyst to help the parties sort through, understand, and evaluate their property/financial situation and develop creative ways to divide assets.

- Child experts or therapists if there are parenting issues that require advice from a professional to address appropriately.

- Appraisers to determine the value of marital assets, such as houses or businesses.

[11.] *Coming to agreements that make sense for the whole family does not require individuals to betray their strongly-held values or feelings. Conscious Divorce Mediators are experts at helping spouses clarify their values and feelings, express them powerfully, and explore creative agreements that allow them to honor those values and feelings while simultaneously ensuring the health of the family going forward.*

- Divorce coaches to help one or both parties stay focused and productive.

- Mortgage lenders to help parties refinance if necessary.

- Other attorneys if a party feels they need additional legal advice or support, such as reviewing agreements before they are signed.

An advantage of the Conscious Divorce Mediation approach is that the divorce team can be as lean or large as the parties feel they need and want to pay for. The parties control the process and the cost, with guidance from the Mediator.

In sum, traditional divorce usually ends up being far more expensive, stressful, and toxic than Conscious Divorce Mediation—and results in a far greater challenge for parents attempting to co-parent after the decree.

The Difference Between Conscious Divorce Mediation and Conventional Mediation

As we've seen, reaching a divorce settlement alone does not necessarily reduce the harmful consequences of divorce. The important thing is reaching an agreement *in a healthy way that stands up long-term and avoids ongoing conflict.* Conscious Divorce Mediation professionals support this goal by (A) identifying specific values that the parties commit to upholding; (B) helping the parties with holistic preparation for the mediation process; (C) skill building; and (D) offering or directing the parties to post-divorce support.

Committing to Values

One of the ways Conscious Divorce Mediation supports a healthy process is to encourage parents to enter into certain commitments up front. For example, participants are typically asked to commit to upholding the following values:

- Transparency

- Focusing on children's interests above all

- Focusing on the future

- Maintaining respect for both adults and their relationship with their children

Transparency means full disclosure of all relevant information to each other and the mediator. Conscious Divorce Mediation relies upon this openness to be effective. The court generally won't approve a settlement if it thinks the parties don't understand the issues or haven't had a chance to review the underlying data.

Making sure the **interests of children** are the highest priority is something most parents can support, even if they're angry with their spouse. However, parents don't always agree on what is in the children's best interests and can temporarily lose sight of their kids' interests when emotionally triggered. The Conscious Divorce Mediation process prepares parents by providing parenting resources, as well as tools to communicate and to stay present and focused on what's most important to them during a time of emotional turmoil.

Focusing on the future means a commitment to thinking long-term and avoiding a scorched-earth mentality. Focus on past behavior and blaming, while understandable, usually only makes a difficult situation worse. On the other hand, many parents discover an incredible sense of empowerment when they can take personal responsibility for the health of their family during and after divorce.

Respect for both adults means valuing the basic well-being and health of both parties. It also means accepting that the Mediator will allow space for each person to be heard. Conscious Divorce mediators understand that each person's perspective is worthy of consideration and respect.

Parties might have other commitments as well, and a Conscious Divorce mediator will ask them what commitments and values they want to bring to the table. Having those commitments in place can be incredibly helpful when emotions start to run high and people tend to forget what is most important. The mediator can support the parties in sticking to their commitments by offering proposals that are consistent with their values, helping the parties stay grounded, and, if necessary, reminding the parties of their commitments if their emotions (understandably) lead them astray.

Preparation

Divorce can be challenging and triggering even under the best circumstances. Parties should get prepared for this challenge by participating in an orientation that provides techniques to help keep spouses calm, centered, and in productive communication.

For example, an orientation session or class should provide the parties with tools such as:

- How to recognize when they are emotionally "triggered" and how to handle the situation when one or both are triggered.

- How to communicate effectively, even when they do not like each other.

- How to stay focused on the future or positive values.

- How to work with difficult emotions in themselves and in their partner and how to stay focused on what is important to them.

- The importance of being accountable.

These tools should be summarized in a poster that is kept visible during all sessions as a reminder to the parties.

Holistic preparation is a hallmark of the Conscious Divorce Mediation process, which often is absent from conventional mediation.

Skill Building

A Conscious Divorce mediator is skillful in modeling conflict-resolution approaches as well as relational communication styles that help couples communicate through difficult situations. Often, people unconsciously create unnecessary conflict simply by how they express themselves to each other. A Conscious Divorce mediator can help the parties engage in powerful, clear, and productive communication that helps them maintain the peace and get what they want.

Post-Divorce Support

If parenting children is hard, post-divorce "co-parenting" is even harder. Parents are suddenly confronted with how to talk to and negotiate with their ex-spouse over child-rearing decisions; how to manage their ex-spouse's anger and resentment and still maintain a good co-parenting relationship; how to maintain flexibility in their parenting arrangements where necessary; and a host of other issues. They can often find the other parent's demands unreasonable and feel like they can't effectively talk to each other about it. Many also have a reasonable fear that their new intimate relationships may exhibit the same problems as the marriage they've just ended.

These issues can be addressed through post-divorce support. No one wants to be in therapy with an ex-spouse, but ongoing support by a Conscious Divorce mediator can help people thrive in their co-parenting relationship, by providing a fresh perspective and offering options to resolve the inevitable disagreements.

How Conscious Divorce Mediation is Related to Conscious Uncoupling and Collaborative Divorce

While Conscious Divorce Mediation shares many values with "Conscious Uncoupling," the focus is somewhat different. Developed by therapist Katherine Woodward Thomas, Conscious Uncoupling is a five-step process that helps an individual use his or her divorce as a time of personal transformation. Conscious Divorce Mediation, in contrast, focuses on shepherding an entire family through divorce in a way that minimizes conflict, helps forge strong agreements, and sets parents up to successfully co-parent after divorce.

Conscious Divorce Mediation also shares many of the principles and values of "Collaborative Divorce." Collaborative Divorce is a formalized process in which each spouse hires a collaboratively trained lawyer. The lawyers are contractually prevented from litigating the case, so if it doesn't settle, the parties must hire new counsel. There is usually also a neutral facilitator/coach, a neutral financial advisor, and potentially other team members such as mortgage professionals or child experts.

In certain cases, it is appropriate to provide individual legal counsel. However, people often find the large Collaborative Divorce team to be prohibitively expensive and cumbersome to coordinate.

Conscious Divorce Mediation resembles the formal "Collaborative" process, in that both include the following:

- Parties of professionals compose a team;
- The team agrees to a set of clear principles and guidelines;
- Out-of-court resolution is reached through a series of settlement meetings; and
- The process is focused on seeking solutions in the best interests of the family as a whole, versus focusing primarily on the legal rights of the individual spouses.

By way of contrast, Conscious Divorce Mediation typically involves a smaller team than collaborative divorce. The Conscious Divorce Mediation team is not established by protocol and can be tailored to meet the parties' particular needs.

Furthermore, the parties are usually not represented by their own lawyers though they may use lawyers sparingly to review agreements and provide strategic advice when needed. Unlike in Collaborative Divorce, any attorney consulted by a party during Conscious Divorce Mediation can represent that party in court if negotiations break down. Fortunately, in our experience, the Conscious Divorce Mediation process rarely ends up with the parties having to resolve anything in court.

Conclusion

Divorcing the wrong way can be emotionally and financially ruinous for an entire family. Until relatively recently, a divorcing couple's only choice was the traditional "lawyer-up and litigate" method. Predictably, given the rules of that game, the result was often far from ideal for families. Traditional divorce is inherently more combative, financially draining, focused on shortsighted goals, inefficient, procedurally lengthy, and harmful to children.

In contrast, Conscious Divorce Mediation provides a positive return on investment (in immediate cost and reduced future conflict and harm), is focused on the long view, is efficient, can be as quick or slow as needed, and is as protective as possible of children.

Divorce need not be a zero-sum game in which each spousal combatant can only gain at the expense of the other's loss. Thankfully, for the sake of our children and the future they represent, more and more people are awakening to the realization that the real prize in divorce is not "winning" from a legal perspective, but preserving the long-term health of their children, and indeed, their entire co-parenting family. Conscious Divorce Mediation is one emerging, powerful method of helping families achieve that prize.

❖

Conscious Divorce Mediators who subscribe to the principles in this chapter may be found in almost every state.

Visit www.consciousfamilylaw.com to learn more.

If you'd like to know if you and your spouse are suited for Conscious Divorce Mediation, or if you should seek to retain a lawyer, complete our free online questionnaire here: www.bit.ly/mediationquiz.

Key Takeaways

- ✓ Research establishes that high conflict during marriage, during divorce, and after divorce devastates the health and well-being of children and parents.

- ✓ Traditional litigated divorce tends to be expensive, lengthy, contentious, and stressful. It often leaves parents financially ruined and ill prepared to move forward as co-parents.

- ✓ Conscious Divorce Mediation is a process that offers an alternative to traditional divorce that saves families money, time, and stress and allows co-parents and their children to thrive after the divorce is complete.

- ✓ Conscious Divorce Mediation can be tailored to meet the unique needs of each family.

ABOUT JOHN C. HOELLE, JD & PETER M. FABISH, JD, MA

John Hoelle and Peter Fabish are co-founders of **Conscious Family - Law & Mediation**, a Boulder, Colorado-based firm with a mission to help people everywhere create and sustain healthy intimate relationships and to collaboratively disentangle when necessary. The firm is composed of family lawyers and mediators who act as advocates, coaches, and mediation experts to help couples in all stages of relationship. Whether couples wish to save or strengthen their relationship, or to transition out of their marriage through divorce, we help families navigate the process of relationship growth and transition.

John is a mediator and Colorado-licensed attorney trained in the Collaborative Divorce model. He has worked under judges and family law litigators, but has no tolerance for attorneys who increase family conflict unnecessarily. When not working with couples or wrestling with his kids, John pursues a personal practice of meditation and yoga and plays electric bass in the kirtan rock band *Bhakti Explosion*.

Peter has served as an attorney and mediator for over two decades. He holds a master's degree in counseling and has practiced as a psychotherapist. Peter has traveled the world to study with a variety of spiritual teachers and masters. When not doing the work he loves, he hikes, bikes, and camps around the mountains and lakes of Colorado with his family.

BUSINESS NAME: Conscious Family Law & Mediation
WEBSITE: www.consciousfamilylaw.com
EMAIL: info@consciousfamilyfirm.com
PHONE: 303.415.2040
LOCATION: Boulder, Colorado
FACEBOOK: www.facebook.com/consciousfamilyfirm
LINKEDIN: www.linkedin.com/in/peterfabish/
www.linkedin.com/in/johnhoelle/
TWITTER: @consciousfmly
AVVO: www.avvo.com/attorneys/80304-co-peter-fabish-20044.html
YOUTUBE: www.youtube.com/channel/UCHrFuzN-HmEUEVJQ7oSAArw

SECTION 2: SECURE YOUR FINANCIAL FUTURE

CHAPTER THREE

THE KEY TO AVOIDING MONEY MISTAKES IN DIVORCE: A DIVORCE FINANCIAL PLANNER

by Kevin R. Worthley, CFP®, CDFA™

"When we have clarity on our destination and are grounded in our current reality, we are equipped to make the best decisions possible."
-Michael Hyatt, Author

Few would argue that the divorce process is, at its best, a tense, unpleasant matter that demands considerable time, effort and often, money. There are also the human emotional costs that are thought to be temporary, but may extend well into the future. While understandable, these emotions may impede making rational, sensible financial decisions in the divorce process. This chapter will explore the various financial issues encountered in divorce mediation and collaborative discussions and why a thorough understanding of these matters (and involving a financial professional) is crucial to future financial success for divorcing spouses.

Over the past decade, mediation and collaborative methods of divorce resolution (often referred to as alternative dispute resolution (ADR) methods), are increasingly preferred over traditional means, such as litigation in the courtroom. This trend is the result of (1) a considerable backlog on the average court docket schedule; (2) the high legal expenses associated with litigation, including preparation, continuances, and other delays; and (3) the recognition that ADR methods can address the emotional and non-material aspects of the divorce process and oftentimes lead to quicker, less expensive, and less emotionally taxing resolutions.

Unfortunately, the money issues may still be complex and not well understood, even in a somewhat cooperative and amiable environment. Further, the money issues in divorce are seldom confined to just what is paid to attorneys or mediators for their counsel and work. In many cases, years, or decades of personal finance within the marriage must now be unwound and divided in a fair and equitable manner. This unwinding normally involves assembling and organizing financial information, evaluating, and discussing the money components that supported the marriage, and negotiating a hopefully amicable agreement between the spouses.

From a purely financial point of view, marriage is an "economic partnership" between spouses and, like a normal business partnership, unwinding and separating the intertwined aspects can be complex and difficult. In many cases, even though the divorce process may be expedited through the services of a mediator or collaborative attorneys, having a financial professional with the tools and expertise in divorce finance can be extremely beneficial to the process and can help clients avoid difficult circumstances later once the settlement has long been agreed upon and implemented.

In our firm's mission statement, we often speak of achieving financial clarity in divorce, whether in discussions between spouses or for the client's own benefit in understanding the financial aspects of this life-change. But what does "clarity" mean? What benefits and understanding will you gain by having a financial professional as part of your divorce team?

Helping clients navigate their way through the money-end of divorce over the years, I've found that most people have only a rudimentary understanding of their financial matters. While attorneys, divorce coaches, counselors, or mediators may be helpful with some financial aspects, these professionals are not fully trained in personal finance to offer more than helpful hints on certain aspects of the big picture. They are certainly not equipped to develop a comprehensive analysis, assist the clients with creating post-divorce budgets, or complete current financial affidavits. Indeed, most are unwilling to do so, since finance is not their area of expertise and they wish to not only avoid professional liability but sincerely want to be sure the information and financial recommendations the clients receive during the process are sound and backed by experience. Thus, without a thorough understanding of all the financial nuances in the divorce situation, decisions may either be made "on the roll of the dice" or via strong negotiation tactics by one spouse and/or their chosen attorney

Divorce is a fact of life today at all income levels. For divorce in low or middle-class households, there is often too much debt, a lack of savings, or insufficient attention to cash-flows. Conversely, for more affluent couples, there may be considerable income and financial assets, but there may also be a higher degree of complexity or, in the case of financial assets and accounts, a wide variety of tax issues, whether such assets are divisible or not, or other matters that make separating these assets more difficult than simply splitting them in half. While the intention is often to divide the marital estate equally, all assets are not created equal. A 50/50 split may be equal, but equal does not necessarily mean "equitable" or fair. In many ways, dividing assets down the middle may look right, but the post-divorce results may be quite different, often years after the final decree has been entered.

There may also be a disparity between spousal incomes, financial assets gained during the marriage, and commonly a wide gap between one spouse's knowledge about the marital money versus the other's awareness. Add an emotionally-charged divorce into this mix and finding acceptable results is usually difficult. Dividing everything involves a myriad of variables and choices. Altering even one of these can have a large effect on either or both post-divorce households.

One reason I devote a portion of my time to divorce finance is the amount of post-divorce planning cases that cross my desk where there have been significant financial mistakes made during the divorce. In many cases, the tax dollars lost to the IRS or the agreements made that put the client in grievous financial straits could have been easily prevented by a little insight, foreknowledge, and understanding of the implications of the financials that were agreed to in the marriage settlement agreement. Had the spouse(s) in these situations fully understood what they were agreeing to and how such terms might affect them post-divorce, one or both may have requested alternative terms or, at the very least, may have been better prepared to adjust their lifestyles well in advance.

A core recommendation I impart to each client is to "not argue over who gets the coffee cup". This is not to say that a spouse should not stand up for what's rightfully theirs or not heed the advice of their chosen attorney to represent their interests. But oftentimes, the emotions that led to the divorce in the first place can get in the way of rational decision-making. As in other aspects of personal finance, high emotions (whether positive or deeply negative) may not lead to sound financial choices.

One key point for divorcing spouses to remember is that they themselves have the power and control over the process, and therefore the cost, of their divorce. Although awareness of the benefits of mediation or collaborative divorce methods to resolution is greater today, there are too many situations that result in unnecessary taxes or high legal fees spent on financially minor differences.

Cash Flow

Cash flows are often a problematic area. In most states, divorcing spouses are required to complete financial affidavits detailing their budgets and income, as well as assets and liabilities. A common issue in these disclosures is that the budget items are often based upon the pre-divorce-marital, not post-divorce-single lifestyles. Although the affidavits are notarized and submitted to the court, these documents are often insufficient as planning tools for the future and can sometimes actually be harmful for negotiating settlement agreements. In other words, how can two spouses determine a workable settlement based upon faulty or inaccurate budgets? We often must ask (and help) clients to recreate their budgets based upon anticipated expenses post-divorce to get a truer picture of what their future anticipated lifestyle may cost them. Accuracy and realism are crucial elements to budgets and affidavits and make analysis and planning effective.

From there (and knowing what is and is not possible for working income, other income, and spousal/child support), cash-flow shortfalls (e.g. income not meeting expenses) are easier to determine and see on a spreadsheet or graph. Trends in shortfalls (with the potential for having to tap future-goal assets to cover the shortfalls, such as IRA and other retirement accounts) can be seen more readily, as are the effects of incorporating alternative solutions and restructuring settlement terms.

Inflation and taxes are two areas of finance that are also underappreciated by most non-financial people. Understanding the effect of these is critical to the survival of one or both spouses in their post-divorce world. Most people don't realize how the rising cost of living can eat away at a person's ability to meet expenses each year. If income is static year to year (or decreases significantly when alimony or child support ends) an unsuspecting divorcee may find themselves far short of money at the end of each month, forcing them to use up savings or retirement assets to make ends meet. Spouses and their chosen mediators/collaborative attorneys should remember that inflation affects purchasing power, or the ability to maintain a given lifestyle over time. One thousand dollars per month in spousal support may be sufficient today, but in 5 years the recipient spouse may find it harder to survive financially.

Taxes

While most people realize that taxes are part of modern life, the effect of taxes on meeting lifestyle expenses or when assets are transferred due to divorce are often not realized, even by the non-financial professionals hired to help with the process. Divorce taxation is a complex subject and not the scope of this chapter, but here are some items to consider:

Transfers of assets between spouses pursuant to divorce generally do not result in taxable events as long as the transfer itself is handled carefully as to not trigger such consequences. That said, spouses and their non-financial advisors need to remember that the cost basis and the potential unrealized appreciation of some assets, such as a house or investment account holdings, carry over to the recipient, who is then responsible for the taxes when the high appreciation is realized and the gain is taxable. This is especially important when transferring ownership of the marital home from joint ownership to just one spouse. If the appreciation in the house rises above $250,000 capital gain exemption over the purchase price, the receiving spouse (single-owner) may thereafter be subject to capital gains tax upon later sale of that home. The second $250,000 or $500,000 total exemption for joint owners is lost when there is just a single homeowner. This tax aspect is often misunderstood in divorce negotiations.

Transfers or divisions of qualified retirement accounts (401k's, etc.) to 'non-participant' spouses are common aspects of divorce, but such transfers must follow strict procedures and be received within IRA Rollover accounts or other such tax-advantaged accounts. Distributions from either the non-spouse 401k account or the later IRA rollover account by the recipient spouse post-divorce is still a taxable (and potentially penalized) event. Only under certain circumstances may a non-participant spouse access 401k-type money for their needs without triggering IRS premature withdrawal penalties.

It is fairly well known that spousal support (alimony) is generally tax-deductible from income by the payer spouse and taxed at ordinary income rates to the payee spouse. What either spouse or their attorneys/mediator may not know is the interplay between the tax aspects of alimony and cash flows, where adjustments to alimony payments and the tax capacity of either the payer or payee might make a divorce financial settlement work. In other words, in certain situations, an increase in alimony might help the payer spouse achieve better tax-planning results while at the same time, the payee spouse has enough after-tax income (being a lower bracket) to meet expenses. Discovery of this solution might only be found through financial analysis by a qualified divorce financial professional.

Retirement pensions are also good examples. Many pension benefits can be divided, however, the payout and use of the pension money may not occur until many years into the future. In addition, there will be an additional legal expense to have a court order (the Qualified Domestic Relations Order, or the QDRO) drafted to instruct the pension administrators of the terms of the division. If there are other retirement assets in the marriage, it may be to the advantage of the non-pensioner spouse to not request a division of the benefit in exchange for more of the other retirement accounts in the asset division, such as IRA accounts, annuities, or other assets where division is less complicated and may be achieved simply with a Letter of Instruction to the custodian of the account along with a copy of the divorce decree.

Understanding the tax characteristics of the assets to be divided is essential, too. Demanding all the tax-deferred assets in a divorce may be a poor decision if those assets must be tapped later for a financial emergency, incurring penalties and taxes in the meantime. Having some of the liquid, non-taxable money might be helpful in the future.

Aside from balance sheets and cash flow statements, however, one aspect of "financial clarity" that we find to be most important is answering a fundamental question: "With this settlement and my new life, will I be all right?" Meaning, of course, after the dust settles and each goes their separate ways, what are the financial implications, especially for the divorcing wife and mother (who often has low or lower income and is usually the custodial parent)? Will she be able to make ends meet? Will she survive financially? Divorce is a scary undertaking. Many women (as well as men) seek reassurance they won't be destitute in their post-divorce life.

Financial Bear Traps Common to Divorce Negotiations

Some financial agreements often lead to problems. One trap could exist with the family residence. If one spouse, say the husband, quit-claims the deed on the house over to his ex-wife but she is unable or not required to refinance the mortgage and get the husband's name off the loan, he is still liable for the debt against it. Any problems or default on the loan could legitimately affect his credit. Similarly, I often see where the spouse remaining in the marital home is wholly unable to afford the expenses of remaining there, even with the mandated child support and (often temporary) alimony. Later, as mentioned previously, if she decides to sell, she may get a nasty tax surprise in the form of capital gains tax. Divorcing couples who need to sell investment property as part of the divorce agreement may run into even nastier depreciation recapture taxes they knew nothing about.

Liquidity is another frequent problem. Does either spouse have enough liquid assets to cover income shortfalls? What if they are overspending their income just to pay the bills? Invading retirement assets could not only create unnecessary federal and state income taxes, but if the ex-spouse is under 59 ½ years old, there are additional penalties to pay as well.

Mistakes are often made by not updating beneficiary designations after the divorce is final. With one situation I witnessed, a divorced woman had failed to change the beneficiary on a substantial medical lawsuit annuity from her ex-husband to her siblings. When she died unexpectedly, guess who got the remaining money? Not the siblings. They were extremely unhappy about the situation but there was nothing they could do.

Similar problems appear in reviewing life insurance policies post-divorce. Unless the beneficiary ex-spouse is the other biological parent of the marital children, most ex-spouses prefer someone other than their ex-spouse to receive the proceeds of their post-divorce life insurance.

Along this line of thought, a crucial area of discussion is insuring the stream of income for spousal and child support from the payer spouse to the payee. This is sometimes an overlooked and problematic aspect of the negotiations from several perspectives:

1) The life (or disability) insurance in place is insufficient or non-existent to provide for the recipient spouse/children, or

2) Provisions to ensure the designated beneficiaries of the policy insuring the payer spouse (and the promised and relied-upon income stream) are indeed the anticipated recipients (ex-spouse/children) and not another person(s) so designated post-divorce.

3) The payer spouse may be uninsurable.

Health insurance is another particular concern. Most settlement discussions do include health insurance, but the laws and options can vary from state to state and are sometimes misunderstood by the spouses and even their attorneys. Due to increasing costs and recent changes in health care, this can be a very complex area.

In Rhode Island, for example, there exists the misconception that the Insurance Continuation Act guarantees that a non-participant ex-spouse must be kept under the employee-spouse's coverage. In fact, the law does not stipulate any such guarantee; it only encourages continuation and outlines what the health insurer may or may not do depending upon the divorce decree. Due to increasing costs of providing healthcare coverage to employees, many private-sector plans may, in fact, exclude ex-spouses from coverage or require such ex-spouses to purchase extended (and expensive) COBRA coverage, even though the children of the marriage may still be included under the employee-parent's plan. In addition, as of January 1, 2014, the spouse of an RI state employee is no longer allowed to remain on the state health insurance program after divorce. This means the ex-spouse will need to find their own health insurance, presumably under the state-sponsored programs administered under the Federal Affordable Care Act if they are not employed or if their own employer does not provide coverage.

In Massachusetts, healthcare is very different. MA law does require employers to allow non-employees to remain on their ex-spouse's healthcare plan, private and municipal, but if the employer is "self-insured", the company may be exempt from MA state law. Even if state law applies, this does not mean ex-spouses won't be required to pay a higher premium. In addition, under Federal tax law, an employer benefit provided to an ex-spouse of an employee (such as healthcare) *is taxable to the employee*! This little-known tax fact and the potential for higher premiums or changes in coverage often require careful analysis and consideration during divorce discussions. It may be crucial, therefore, for an advisor such as a CDFA™ or an attorney to review what options the healthcare plan offers to divorcing spouses.

College Financial Considerations

It's no secret that college costs are rising at alarming rates and causing an increasing amount of financial difficulty for both students and their parents. Being aware of the impact divorce has on college financial aid and financing is vital.

Family cash-flow during the college years, financial aid, and the ability (or not) to meet the Estimated Family Contribution (EFC) are all factors that are heavily influenced by divorce. Given some cooperation and planning by the divorcing parents, they, and their student(s) may avoid costly mistakes and benefit from a properly-structured divorce settlement.

Unless they themselves have immersed themselves in the college finance and financial aid arena for their own children, few mediators or collaborative attorneys have the experience to advise their divorcing clients on the nuances of college funding or how divorce affects financial aid eligibility. In addition, family law statutes in many states do not include provisions for requiring divorcing parents to provide for college expenses later. Nevertheless, with the potentially immense financial burden that comes with sending children to college (for married as well as divorced parents), it is crucial to include this topic within the mediated or collaborative divorce discussion. Since it is common for both parents to want their children to attend college, having such discussions in a cooperative environment for divorce may yield benefits to both the custodial family and the non-custodial parent.

The first step is having a solid grasp of the financial aid system and eligibility process. Many financial advisors have little to no knowledge of how financial aid is calculated. Without knowing how the financial aid formulas work and the criteria for income and assets, planners may be making recommendations that hurt the family's eligibility for aid. A common example is custodial accounts. What the planner may not realize is that UGMA/UTMA accounts are considered assets of the student-beneficiary, not the custodial parent, and therefore are assessed 20-25% of value in the aid formulas instead of the maximum 5.6% effective rate for parent assets. Mistakes like this could potentially cost the family thousands of dollars in lost aid.

It is also important to know there are two Estimated Family Contribution formulas, the Federal Methodology (FM) and the Institutional Methodology (IM). These calculations are similar but also have major differences. The FM is calculated using the information on the FAFSA form, which is a general "once-over-lightly" of the family's income and assets. Used by most public college and some private schools, the FM excludes home equity and retirement accounts and allows the family to shelter a portion of their assessable assets. Under the Institutional Method (IM), however, used by most private colleges, home equity is counted to some degree and there are no student income shelters.

For financial aid calculations in a divorce situation, most colleges (especially the public schools) usually only consider the "custodial family" of the student. The custodial parent is generally the one with whom the student has resided more than 50% of the year, (i.e. 183 nights under whose roof in a calendar year). This means the non-custodial parent may not have his/her income or assets as part of the aid calculations. Private schools requiring the CSS Profile financial aid application will ask for the non-custodial parent's financials, however.

There may be a significant difference in the financial resources between the two biological parents, and ideally, the student could potentially benefit by being the custodial child of the parent with the lower income and lower assessable assets. Parents should be careful, though, as a parent with higher income and assets may also have more obligations that may lower their net EFC below that of the other parent. In the case of second marriages, it's also crucial to know that the income and countable assets of a step-parent residing in the custodial home are indeed counted as part of the household and step-siblings are counted as a member of the student's household if they reside with the student.

Many times, a student's chosen private college will request financial information on the non-custodial parent, who then balks and refuses to provide tax returns and asset and income information. This is due to fears the college may require contributions from that parent that were not part of the divorce agreement. What many parents fail to realize is that colleges only assess certain assets in the aid calculations, and even then, the percentage of value assessed of those assets are very low, often only 3-4%. Home equity and retirement accounts are often not a factor, especially for most public colleges.

Eligibility for college financial aid may be significantly impacted by the terms of the divorce decree on the division of income and assets. For example, whether a custodial parent receives qualified or non-qualified accounts as part the marital asset division can affect financial aid eligibility. Acquired non-qualified assets may be counted to some degree over sheltered amounts whereas qualified accounts (employer-sponsored retirement accounts and IRA's) are not counted in the formulas. Of course, other considerations such as liquidity needs of the custodial family must be taken into consideration.

Income plays an important role as well. Since parental and custodial income is generally the primary factor in the college aid formulas, if college is imminent for the custodial family, structuring spousal support to coincide with aid application years could be beneficial. As an example, since parental income is more highly assessed in the Federal formula, a lower-earning custodial parent whose child is considering a local public university might accept more non-retirement account assets in the settlement in lieu of higher spousal support so greater eligibility for college financial aid for the student might be possible (the custodial parent, therefore, draws down on the awarded accounts for income instead of alimony during the college years), since parental assets are assessed at a maximum 56% of value versus the much higher assessment on parental income (20-25%) toward the Estimated Family Contribution.

Since both college and divorce are complex areas of financial planning that demand specific knowledge of many items that could significantly affect making proper recommendations, it is beneficial to the discussion to have the input of a knowledgeable financial professional.

Conclusion

Even if the marital finances are not so complicated, many divorcing people may feel better knowing that the solutions have been reviewed from an objective point of view. If the solution and outcome aren't as rosy as hoped for, at least all the rocks have been looked under. A divorce financial analyst planner can play a critical role in ensuring that a best-possible outcome can be reached between the parties and assist the mediation/collaborative team in understanding the financial aspects of the divorce. To summarize, a divorce financial analyst can:

- Assist the parties in determining realistic post-divorce objectives and lifestyles.

- Work to ensure the financial data (assets/liabilities/budgets/other data) is accurate and understood between the parties.

- Help the parties understand what is financially workable and possible for the marriage settlement agreement.

- Provide insight and understanding about the potential long-term financial outcomes of one proposal versus another and show why a particular solution may or may not be advantageous to one or both parties.

- Assist the ADR professionals in creating a workable atmosphere, and promote a more effective, time/expense-efficient resolution process.

- Help the divorcing parties avoid calamitous financial mistakes and better assurance that the final agreement will result in a financially workable post-divorce future.

Finally, financial clarity and analysis offer a reality check. Uncertainty, fear, and doubt are negative emotions that can cause paralysis in divorce. Once the financials have been dissected and probable solutions have been considered, people are usually relieved and more confident about their futures. Even if the results are not what they've hoped for, often they are also not as bad as they had feared. In the end, clarity can mean confidence and encouragement that a satisfying, if not enjoyable, post-divorce life is indeed possible.

❖

For more information on divorce financial planning and its benefits, visit www.equitable-divorce-solutions.com or email Kevin directly:

kevin@equitable-divorce-solutions.com.

Key Takeaways

✓ There are a variety of financial issues encountered in divorce mediation and collaborative discussions.

✓ A thorough understanding of these financial issues is critical to your financial success.

✓ Involving a financial professional will give you peace of mind and help you sort out and comprehend the financial issues common in a divorce.

ABOUT KEVIN R. WORTHLEY, CFP®, CDFA™

Kevin Worthley is a Certified Financial Planner® practitioner and a Certified Divorce Financial Analyst (CDFA™). He graduated from the University of Miami with a BA in Economics in 1984. He has extensive experience and expertise in college and divorce matters and has been helping clients in Rhode Island and Massachusetts with divorce financial analysis and planning for over 14 years.

Kevin is a member and a past Board Director of the Rhode Island Chapter of the Financial Planning Association, a past Board Director of the Association of Divorce Financial Planners (ADFP), and a member of the Rhode Island Mediators Association. Since 2001, he has written a bi-weekly personal finance column for the Newport Daily News in Newport, Rhode Island, as well as articles on divorce finance for the Rhode Island Women's Journal. Kevin has been quoted in the national media on issues regarding divorce planning, appearing on Fox Business News, Forbes.com, NBCNews.com, and Reuters.com.

BUSINESS NAME: Equitable Divorce Solutions, LLC
WEBSITE: www.equitable-divorce-solutions.com
EMAIL: kevin@equitable-divorce-solutions.com
PHONE: 401.842.8151
LOCATION: North Smithfield, RI

CHAPTER FOUR

How to Construct Mutually Advantageous Divorce Financial Agreements: Eight Anecdotal Illustrations

by William M. Morris, CDFA™

A philosopher once commented on unhappiness stating, "Life is too short to live like that!" For those who have been in a really bad marriage, our view is, "Life is too long to live like that." It's your choice... We can help!

"Let them eat cake!" Marie Antoinette was quoted as saying in 1789 in response to the statement that children in the streets were hungry with no bread to eat. Although she probably didn't say this, there is no doubt she was out of touch with the common people starving in the streets–especially the children.

Combative attorneys with high fees drain the marital estate at an alarming rate while "fighting for your rights." They are out of touch with what today's families need. "We'll make him pay," retorts the divorce attorney advertising on TV, with the same level of veracity as Marie Antoinette.

Variations of both positions damage the divorce process, including the adults and children abused by the lawyers and combatants in a traditional divorce.

There must be a better way—we know there is a better way!

I have invested over 30 years of my professional life to helping clients find better ways to run their businesses and organize their financial lives. The experience of working with individuals to improve their businesses, their financial well-being, and their personal goals lead me to become a founding member of the East Tennessee Collaborative Alliance.

Our goal is to construct less destructive divorce agreements that include detailed financial plans, guiding clients towards a positive future. Our practice includes lawyers, financial planners, and mental health professionals trained in both the collaborative process and mediation. Our holistic approach guides families to a kinder, gentler, comprehensive divorce agreement.

I would like to claim we have a 100% success rate—we do not. Sometimes there are elements within the divorce process that simply cannot be resolved through our cooperative process. Sometimes logical minds simply disagree. At those times, we must rely on our training as mediators to help our clients make the hard decisions.

The basic guidelines of mediators and collaborative professionals are very much alike. Both professions assist people going through the divorce make their own decisions with our input. In this context, collaborative professionals provide a more open-ended analysis of the elements of divorce and encourage the participants to develop their own conclusions. When an impasse is confronted, rather than continuing to debate with lawyers and advisors on the clock, it is often more prudent to take the narrowly defined disagreement to arbitration.

In our practice, that means the arbitrator will help to objectively define the problem and the various options proposed to dissolve the issue. Should the two parties not be able to resolve the dispute in question, the arbitrator will propose a distinct solution and work to obtain acceptance by both parties—even if both parties are not in total agreement. It is important to remember that in most divorces, not everyone gets everything they initially think they are due.

Sometimes, even when both parties agree on the division of assets, a disagreement on how assets are divided can threaten to derail the process or the division can be structured such as to harm one or both parties.

To help you think about how different financial agreements can be structured, consider the following anecdotes. They may not apply to your exact situation; however, they help illustrate how viewing possible outcomes from different angles can often lead to a better agreement. This is easier to do when you have a trained financial planner on your divorce team.

The Tax Man Cometh

The Internal Revenue Service is not very sympathetic to divorce. Whether your divorce is final on January 1st or the day after Christmas, the IRS will consider you divorced for the entire year. You will not be relieved of responsibility for past year's tax payments should the IRS revisit a previous filing.

I had a previous tax deduction challenged and finally reversed from a tax filing seven years prior to my divorce. I stressed to the IRS that my divorce decree specified we would be jointly responsible and they needed to contact my ex-wife for her half. Their response was that they were going to extract the back taxes (plus interest) from me and I could go to court to get my ex's portion. While we were negotiating payment, the IRS seized my business bank account! They play rough. Be sure you understand the impact divorce may have on current and past joint filings with the IRS.

After the divorce, you will need to file as single or head of household. If you and your former spouse have significant differences in income, you may require negotiation. Filing status and claimed dependents may be more beneficial to one party and should be explored.

Selling your home before you are divorced may be beneficial from a tax standpoint. An individual can receive a $250,000 exclusion for profit in the sale of their personal residence. That means you can avoid taxes on your profit up to $500,000 if you are married. If one of you sells the home after the divorce, you lose one-half of the exclusion. At a 15% tax on long-term gains, that's an additional $37,500 in taxes. Ouch! Timing is important.

On the other hand, if there is going to be a significant difference in tax brackets between you and your ex after the divorce, optimizing tax considerations in asset transfer can provide more money to the receiving party at lower after-tax costs to the payer. A recent client paid significantly more over time, but saved $250,000 after taxes!

Home Sale Ménage-a-Trois

Mary and Tom bought a home on the beach at auction for $200,000 fifteen years ago. The current value of the home is over $1,000,000. The couple is now divorcing. Pursuant to their divorce decree, they have agreed that Mary can stay in the home until Tom, Jr. goes off to college. Six months later, Mary finds a new love and she and Bob are married. Three years later, Tom, Jr. is 18 and leaves for college. The home is put on the market and sells for a net $1,200,000. How much of the profit is taxable?

A. $1,000,000

B. $750,000

C. $500,000

D. $250,000

Mary can use the $250,000 personal exclusion since Mary satisfies the ownership (5 years) and occupancy (2 years) requirements. Tom can use the $250,000 personal exclusion since the property was titled in both their names (5-year ownership) and he gets credit for Mary's occupancy since the arrangement was pursuant to the divorce. Bob can also claim a $250,000 personal exclusion because only one of the married couple needs to meet the ownership requirements. Thus, answer D is correct. Only $250,000 is taxable of Tom's $500,000 share of the long-term gains.

Sometimes More is Less

Taxes can have a significant impact on tax-deferred accounts such as retirement funds. If Tom and Mary have a $100,000 tax-deferred account and Tom is in the 39.6% tax bracket and Mary is in the 15% tax bracket, can you see the difference? The account is worth $60,400 to Tom and $85,000 to Mary. That's a rough generalization, but you can see there is a significant after-tax difference.

Spousal support or alimony is treated as income to the receiving party and a tax deduction for the paying party. As highlighted above, the difference in tax brackets between divorcing parties is often seen as a tax saving strategy to transfer assets. The IRS has strict rules on how payments can be categorized as support and tax-deductible. The IRS is suspicious if you attempt to transfer large amounts of assets as alimony to take the tax deduction. There can be significant tax savings, but it is important to review the options with your advisor to ensure everything will pass IRS muster.

WILLIAM M. MORRIS · 67

Enough is Enough

Tom and Mary are divorcing after 20 years. Tom is ordered to pay Mary alimony of $20,000 per year for three years so she can get her feet back under her. It was a contentious divorce and Tom hates the thought of writing a check every month to Mary. He negotiates with her attorney to pay her $55,000 up front to be shed of his responsibility. (Tom is in the 33% tax bracket and figures his net cost is $36,850) Mary likes the idea of getting her money today and is willing to take around 8% less.

Problem: Alimony payments in excess of $15,000 are subject to possible recapture (of taxes) if the amount paid drops by more than $15,000 over the first three years. Mary will be able to take a deduction and Tom will have to add the recapture of $40,000 taxable income to their respective tax returns for the third year.

How could they have avoided the tax problem?

a) Tom and Mary could have agreed to characterize the $55,000 as a settlement payment. Tom would not get a tax deduction and Mary would not report the money as income—a clean break.

b) Tom could open a brokerage account and put the money in a money market account with instructions that $20,000 per year be transferred to Mary's bank account. There might be fees involved, but the interest on the money would offset some of the expenses and Tom would not have to deal with Mary. Tom can increase the payments to Mary so her net is still $60,000 while saving money on an after-tax basis. Let's let Uncle Sam chip in.

House or Home?

The home is typically one of a divorcing couple's largest financial assets and involves the greatest amount of emotional anxiety. Should you keep your home or sell it? Consider the following questions:

- Is it in your children's best interests to stay in the home?

- Can you afford the mortgage, taxes, insurance, and maintenance?

- How stressful is the atmosphere in your home?

Although you may love your home and neighborhood, bear in mind that a house is a very costly, illiquid asset. The mortgage, real estate taxes, capital gains taxes, utility bills, insurance, and maintenance can add up over time. Will you be able to afford the house once the marriage is dissolved? You will need to analyze your budget, project your expenses, examine your mortgage options, and review financial information that may assist you in determining whether you should negotiate to keep the house. Can you afford to keep the house?

Most people can readily identify their main household expenses: mortgage payments, insurance, utilities, and housekeeping. What may be overlooked is deferred maintenance—how old is the roof, the water heaters, the air conditioning units, appliances, carpets, wall painting, etc.? Will you need to buy additional furniture or appliances post-divorce?

With interest rates at all-time lows, many people think they will refinance their house to pay for upgrades and/or reduce monthly payments. The problem is that any support you may receive post-divorce will not be considered income for mortgage qualifications. Ben Bernanke, former head of the Federal Reserve, had a mortgage application rejected because he was unemployed, even though he was being paid over $100,000 for speaking engagements!

Even if you want to downsize, you may not be able to qualify for a new mortgage. You may be limited to what you can afford to buy for cash or you may need to enter the rental market.

Whose Business is It?

Tom spent the last ten years building his business working long hard hours. He took all the risks and his spouse stayed home and cared for their home and children. It's his business and his soon-to-be-ex has no rights to the business. Right?

Wrong. The courts see Tom and Mary's marriage as a partnership. All assets accumulated in the period they were married are marital assets unless they were maintained in a separate manner. To be excluded, the assets must have been properly titled and kept separate for the duration of the marriage. The rules are very specific.

If you owned an asset or earned a benefit before you were married, but the value increased during your marriage, a portion of that asset may be classified as a marital asset subject to division. In general, a mathematical ratio is applied called the Coverture Fraction. This simply means if you were married a portion of the time you built your business (married six out of ten years for example), then 60% of the value of that business is marital property. The Coverture Fraction does not take into consideration the fact that the real growth in your business only occurred in the last two years. If so, litigation is probably in your future. If you were the spouse that was not involved in this business, you're in luck. The courts understand that your support of the marriage added value to the development of this business. You have a recognized interest in the value of the business.

You can either buy out your spouse or become/welcome a new partner in your business. You could not get along in your marriage, what chance is there that you could survive as partners?

The IRS Can Help

Recently, I had a case that involved a stockbroker and his young wife. He just wanted to write a check for $1,000,000 and be done with the process. Under no condition did he want to pay alimony. However, Because of the disparity in income tax brackets, he was better off paying her alimony of $1,300,000 over seven years. The alimony was tax deductible and he would have needed to earn over $1,500,000 to have enough after-tax cash to settle the divorce his way. But in this model, Uncle Sam kicked in the extra $300,000 for her. (*Don't hold me to these exact numbers.*) Sometimes a deep dive into assets, income, and attitudes can yield surprising options.

Let's Make a Deal

One of the advantages of collaborative divorce is total disclosure of assets by all parties. After all, 2 plus 2 equals 4. Right? Wrong! Maybe? What if it's really 5 or 5.25 and it makes more sense for Mary to receive 3.25 while Tom keeps 2.0? Who determines the value of the asset and how much is marital? Is there a more tax advantageous method than a 50/50 split on the day of the divorce? If all assets are not split on the final court date, what guarantees are there that the agreement will be completed on time? Same for alimony, how is it paid? What protects the cash flow? What if the payer is disabled or killed?

Once you've identified all your marital assets, it's time to decide who gets what. Your financial advisor (CDFA™) should be able to demonstrate several models allocating assets along an equitable divide. There will be assets you have an emotional attachment to, and you should speak up and express your desire to put those assets on your side of the ledger. It is rare for everyone to get all the assets they want. Some compromise is required. If you have a painting worth $5,000 you want to keep, you must be ready to move an item of similar value to your ex's column—or cash! Even in a litigated divorce, the more you can agree on the better.

I read a recent marriage dissolution agreement (MDA) that had been settled by the court. The couple had been through quite a battle, but they could not come to an agreement on the amount of money the wife should receive or how to transfer her share of the marital assets in the husband's business. The reason I was involved was that the MDA had a calculation error in it made by the judge that neither attorney caught until the agreement had been signed, sealed, and delivered. The parties were exhausted and left the details up to the attorneys. The attorneys were busy clapping each other on the back for reaching an agreement and totaling up their bills to the clients.

The wife's attorney was filling out an order for modification to send back to the court because a calculation error by the judge left the wife $220,000 short. There were a couple other aspects of the MDAs that boggled my mind:

1) The judge determined the financial award based on his belief that the wife should be able to earn a net return of 5% on her portion of the settlement. I've only been a financial advisor for 25 plus years, so maybe that's why I don't know where anyone can earn 5% after taxes on a safe, secure investment in our current financial market.

2) The judge ordered the husband to exercise his company's line of credit to borrow $750,000 to pay his ex for her interest in the business. He forced him to put his company at risk and go into debt to satisfy the MDA!

The collaborative process is a great strategy for a low-conflict, agreeable result—even though the process is not without financial challenges. The financial neutral's responsibility, whether a CDFA™ or mediator, includes discovery of assets, financial modeling of each parties' needs, and then presenting various models to meet the future needs of both parties and their children. Rather than a legal determination of asset distribution, our responsibility is to develop the most financially feasible solution for all parties. Sometimes less is more, even when both parties feel more is not enough.

I hope these anecdotes have encouraged you to collaborate, mediate, or utilize give-and-take to negotiate your terms before you hire a warrior and go to court. Give the judge something he can rule on. Don't ask him to function as a CPA, Financial Advisor, or business consultant. Most are not trained in those disciplines. Remember, most judges were lawyers first and had limited financial training in law school.

Consider the following questions and review with your attorney's guidance:

- How much money will you need to maintain your current standard of living?

- How much will you ask for?

- How much are you willing to pay?

- If you request too much, will it delay settlement resulting in costly litigation?

- What is the minimum settlement that you are willing to accept?

I know from personal experience that the thrill of leaving the courthouse a "free" man was tempered with all the tasks ahead to complete my divorce and begin my single life. Make sure your financial responsibilities are taken care of in a way that is agreeable to both parties with the help of a qualified financial neutral to ensure you're ready for life post-divorce.

❖

Simplify and organize your divorce process by downloading our pre-divorce and post-divorce checklists. You can also order a copy of our 115-page *Divorce Financial Planning Guide.* Both can be found on our website here:

www.easttennesseecollaborative.com/documents

Key Takeaways

- ✓ Separate *wants* from *needs*.
- ✓ The shortest route to your goal may not be a straight line.
- ✓ Good financial advice costs less than errors in your settlement.
- ✓ You cannot look to the future until your divorce is behind you.

ABOUT WILLIAM M. MORRIS, CDFA™

Bill has over 25 years of experience as a business consultant and financial advisor. He is a Senior Wealth Strategy Associate with an international brokerage firm. He holds the Certified Divorce Financial Analyst and Advanced Divorce Financial Analyst designation from the Institute for Divorce Financial Analysts™ and is a listed Rule 31 Mediator in the field of Family Mediation with the Tennessee Supreme Court. Bill is also a founding member and officer of the East Tennessee Collaborative Alliance (etca.us) and featured columnist of *The Bottom Line* for the East Tennessee Medical News. He has produced monthly CLE classes for attorneys and CE classes for allied professionals since 2012, incorporating his 107-page *Divorce Financial Planning Guide,* first published in 2013.

BUSINESS NAME: East Tennessee Collaborative Alliance
WEBSITE: www.etca.us
EMAIL: bill.morris@ubs.com
PHONE: 865.310.3030
LOCATION: Knoxville, TN
LINKEDIN: www.linkedin.com/in/susanandbillmorris
PROFESSIONAL SITES:
Morris Financial Group
www.financialservicesinc.ubs.com/team/morris
East Tennessee Collaborative Alliance
www.easttennesseecollaborative.com/professionals/bill-morris

SECTION 3: DON'T GO THROUGH IT ALONE

THE SECRET TO PROTECTING YOUR KIDS FROM DIVORCE FALL-OUT: THE COLLABORATIVE CHILD SPECIALIST

by Ria Severance, LMFT

"Only because we are the lifeboats for our children, do they sense with merciless acuity the places in us that leak, and then throw themselves, body and soul, into those thin, punctured spots where our capacity to Love remains compromised . . . to see if, in the face of our real frailties, we will muster the courage to Love ourselves and them enough to grow in the ways that make Love stay."
-Ria Severance

Understanding What's "Normal" in a Divorce: An Empathetic View

Divorce is commonplace, it is nevertheless a traumatic life crisis for most families. Stress may be at an all-time high for all family members, as they experience ongoing losses and wonder how the chips will fall for their futures. They often feel isolated while in each other's presence. Even the unspoken tensions, distrust, and hostilities between divorcing parents significantly rock the worlds of their children.

Neuroscience is clear that whenever either children or adults are distressed or upset, their forebrains shut down (the part of the brain that reasons, plans, and considers ethical issues and the long-term effects of a given behavior). When distressed, the brain switches from forebrain neural circuitry to the lower brain stem, the instinctual part of the brain that focuses on fundamental survival—fight, flight, freeze, or fawn. Consequently, reasoning, planning, and ethics are not easily undertaken during a crisis. For divorcing parents, the physiological effect is the same whether there is a saber-toothed tiger in the room, or your co-parent calls and threatens to quit working to get back at you for wanting spousal support. When young children experience even unspoken tension during a divorce, there may be more frequent meltdowns, acting out of aggression, or defiance over seemingly trivial issues. Teens are surprisingly similar. Typically, members of a family that are restructuring due to divorce simply do not function as well as they did before.

Parents are the "context," the touchstone for their kids. Consequently, when the parental foundation is destabilized, kids are destabilized. Finances that once sustained one household must now support two. Children may have to shuttle, often between one smaller home and another. They may not be able to continue at their current school if tuition is an issue or if parents have to move to a different school district for new employment or for more affordable housing. Thus, kids may lose their schools, social support systems, extracurricular activities, homes, neighborhoods, and diversions at the same time they lose their intact family.

Parents going through a divorce are almost never at their best. They may be depressed, irritable, distracted, overwhelmed, intensely fearful, anxious, angry, and emotionally unavailable. Awful as this is, it is "normal." Amidst a divorce, parents may violate parent-child boundaries by treating their children as confidants, mediators, or advocates. Stay-at-home parents may have to find employment outside the home, grieve the loss of time with their kids, and struggle to readjust their identities as caretakers while fearing their job skills are no longer relevant to the workplace. They may have to be less physically available to their children—yet another loss.

Without the primary caregiver's acting as a bridge to the children, primary breadwinners may not know how to effectively engage the kids on their own and may be at a loss about how to connect and parent in ways that are effective, supportive, and meaningful for their children. Both parents may fear a loss of access to their kids, falling out of favor, or worse, fear being actively alienated from their children by a devaluing co-parent. In short, insecurities that may not have been present before the divorce easily become salient in the midst of one. Parenting skills missing before the divorce are now more urgently needed.

I speak not only as an experienced Collaborative Divorce Professional but as a divorced mother of two. I had 20+ years of solid clinical experience and interpersonal skills training and excellent relationship skills in all areas of my life. Then I went through my divorce. In the midst of the crisis, I was not the mother I had been, and I was horrified—which made things worse. As if the process weren't hard enough, guilt, doubt and self-blame abound for divorcing parents.

Recent studies at UCLA indicate that approximately 93% of our communication is nonverbal, so our kids "get" the unspoken tension, hostility, etc. between co-parents. We may manage to significantly limit the damage by holding our tongues about or to our co-parent in front of them, but our children still experience what is unsaid. Our petty shames and fears float furiously to the surface, although we may not speak of them or even let *ourselves* know clearly what we are thinking. Divorcing parents often report thoughts like:

- "My co-parent will be able to take the kids out to fancy dinners, movies, and concerts. Will they want to be with me, if I can't?"

- "Will they know me as the 'poor parent'?"

- "I've been at work. I don't even know my kids. What will I do with them?"

- "I'm going to buy them stuff and let them do whatever they want so they'll want to be with *me*."

- "I actually feel some relief when the kids disrespect or devalue my co-parent."

- "I've made sure my children will qualify for top colleges, now I have to tell them they can't go because *I* can't afford to pay my half of the cost? They'll think *I'm* the obstacle to their success!"

If parents are the foundation, kids often find themselves standing on the quicksand of parental insecurities during a divorce.

Co-parents often fear for their own future wellbeing and for the loss of control over the wellbeing of their children. How will they explain the drop-in resources available to their children? Too often, the loss of income is explained by blaming the co-parent: "If your dad were willing to share what he has, we could . . ." Even after divorce, some co-parents may fear being at the mercy of an unsafe, unstable, self-serving, and/or exploitative co-parent and may fear the same for their children. For some kids, the "favored" co-parent may demonize or actively undermine their relationship with the rejected parent, e.g. by threatening to cut the child off financially if they endorse the devalued parent in some way.

When I say "children" here, I include children over the age of 18. In more divorce cases than I can count, adult children are pulled into the middle of their parents' disputes. Children are used as mediators, are pressured to take sides, and walk on pins and needles as they anxiously navigate who will take them out after their college graduations, who will have the baby shower at their house, etc. These adult kids suffer. And without effective intervention and co-parenting help, the tension often continues for the rest of their lives.

While divorce is a life crisis, you will get through this one step at a time. You can—and will—do what needs to be done to the best of your ability. There are genuinely compassionate, committed, and highly skilled professionals out there to help you keep moving forward in a way that's affordable as well as aligned with your values. You have every reason to believe you can get through this divorce and be stronger and wiser than you were before. You can learn to enhance the quality of your relationship with yourself, your kids, and others.

What is a Collaborative Child Specialist (CS)?

Collaborative Divorce provides a kinder divorce option for separating parents and helps them move forward by focusing on their co-parenting roles and skills. Including a Collaborative Child Specialist on the divorce team helps you remain mindful of the wellbeing of the children while making divorce-related decisions. While you and your co-parent are in turmoil, the CS aligns with your highest values to ensure the children have an age-appropriate voice, as well as an advocate for their best interests and concerns. Involving a CS is one of the best ways you help to protect your children from divorce fall-out.

The Collaborative Child Therapist (CS) is a licensed mental health professional equipped with an understanding of children's various developmental stages and the impact of divorce on children at those stages. The CS informs and updates the Divorce Coaches working with each parent, throughout a collaborative divorce.

At the very outset of a Collaborative Divorce, Divorce Coaches guide parents to prepare and agree to a "Mission Statement" for the divorce process—usually 2-4 sentences that speak to the co-parents' highest values, including the wellbeing of their children. Throughout the collaborative divorce, all professional team members call on this mission statement to help redirect the divorcing couple's focus and bring them back to what is most important to them.

Typically, Divorce Coaches facilitate parents' developing co-parenting skills as they create a parenting plan that considers the defined needs of the children, as well as parental constraints (e.g. work hours, available funds for children). The CS weighs in on the forging of a parenting plan after meeting with the children to assess and address specific emotional and practical day-to-day challenges that arise out of the divorce. When children are already in therapy, the CS may confer by phone with their therapist(s) and meet for as little as an hour with each child before one or more joint meetings with parents and their Divorce Coaches. When parents are more contentious and emotionally volatile about shared parenting, the CS and Divorce Coaches may need significantly more time to work with the family.

Collaborative Child Specialists and Divorce Coaches often request that parents bring in photos of their children that are placed in the middle of the workspace during collaborative meetings. These photos help remind parents of how crucial it is that their love for their children, rather than their immediate personal desires and hurts, guides their decisions about the parenting plan and the restructuring of their family.

When functioning as a co-mediator, I have needed as little as 1.5 hours with some parents to generate a parenting plan. Others have required numerous 2-hour meetings. The cost of a collaborative divorce depends significantly on the parents' ability to communicate effectively and manage their emotions. Co-parenting, emotional regulation, and communication skills are taught and managed throughout a collaborative divorce. These skills empower parents to get through the divorce more efficiently, to minimize conflict, and to reduce parental distress, which relieves stress on their children. Parents with improved skills also interact more effectively long after the divorce.

To help high-conflict parents avoid seeking costly legal solutions to relational problems, even *litigating* family law attorneys refer their clients to collaboratively-trained mental health professionals for co-parenting work. When *two* collaboratively-trained, co-parenting specialists work together with two high-conflict parents, the added support can increase the effectiveness of the process. High-conflict co-parents may finally be able to communicate sufficiently to allow their litigating attorneys to negotiate agreements, instead of litigating parenting plans and other divorce-related disputes, thus saving a fortune in legal fees.

Although Divorce Coaches and CS's are licensed mental health professionals, their goal is not your healing or that of your children, as it is in therapy. Instead, the goal is to get you to the divorce finish line as respectfully and efficiently as possible. They also aim to provide you and your family with the tools you need to develop and sustain healthier relationships in your post-divorce life. When strife is likely to continue to adversely impact the children after the divorce, the CS will often recommend therapy for children and parents and/or refer parents for additional work with co-parenting specialists.

Selecting the Right CS for Your Family

When choosing an effective Collaborative Child Specialist, look for a professional who eases the way for your children, helps you remain mindful of their best interests, and supports your enhancing the quality of your relationship with them amidst any ongoing turmoil. Select a CS who:

- Starts from the assumption that you love your children and are doing the best you can, no matter how harshly *you* may judge your own or your co-parent's skills at the moment.

- Is consistently nonjudgmental. The CS systematically avoids endorsing or aligning with ineffective parenting behaviors, being pulled into alliances with one parent against another, and blaming or judging.

- Identifies, affirms, and builds on your strengths, those of your co-parent (no matter how inept you think your co-parent may be), and the strengths of your children.

- Provides creative solutions to parenting challenges and sustains strong relationships with collaborative team professionals who support creative solutions.

- Articulates in a way that creates an empathic bridge between each parent and the children, as well as between fearful parents.

- Has the courage and strength to actively block, contain, and set limits with parents who act out impulsively in meetings.

- Focuses on skill building which helps reduce judgmental attitudes, criticism, and blaming. A CS trained to teach emotion regulation, distress tolerance/impulse-control, mindfulness, and interpersonal effectiveness can empower children to learn these skills throughout the divorce process.

3 Shortsighted Reasons for Not Using a CS

The Collaborative Child Specialist is the most frequently excluded member of a collaborative divorce team—a shortsighted decision. Here are three faulty, common, and interrelated reasons used to justify excluding the CS.

Cost

Most early Collaborative Divorce models always included a CS. Too often, a CS isn't hired onto the collaborative team because parents or other team members fear the additional cost. This can be detrimental to the overall divorce process. A neutral CS, respected by both parents as an advocate for their children, is often the one professional who can pull parents off their rigid positions and towards their highest values—values often called forth by concern for the wellbeing of their children. The CS represents the children's voices but remains neutral with the parents. This neutrality can reduce tensions and help the entire collaborative team move through an entrenched impasse towards agreement. The CS can increase efficiency and thereby reduce costs.

When there is no CS, a coach-initiated focus on the kids is easily experienced as an unsolicited intrusion. Without a neutral representative for the kids, a parent may be dismissive or feel betrayed and even angry when collaborative team members attempt to raise legitimate concerns about the children.

Lack of Understanding

A second obstacle is that some co-parents and collaborative teams fail to understand how the absence of a CS negatively impacts the divorce process as well as the children's long-term development. Without a CS, Divorce Coaches may be hard pressed to provide a valid focus on the children.

I recall one case in which parents firmly rejected the need for a CS given that one child was 18 and the other 21. The entire professional team could have remedied this by staying faithful to the need for a CS. In this case, both highly successful, educated parents consistently used the kids as mediators and as leverage to argue for what they wanted. Their formulaic approach was: "Jane wants me/us to do X. Given this child's endorsement, I 'should' get to do X." This dynamic violates a healthy parent-child boundary and assumes it is acceptable to burden kids with knowing about and dictating the terms of their parents' divorce.

The presence of a neutral CS provides *an explicit call to action regarding the wellbeing of children.* In this case, despite our best efforts as coaches, the parents were unwilling to engage our concerns for their kids. Even with support from other team professionals, our "coach" roles could not mandate our advocating for the children. When we tried, these co-parents dismissed us or viewed us as imposing our personal agendas. Only the presence of a neutral CS could have justified that advocacy. Consequently, for the rest of their lives these adult children will most likely continue to be used by their parents to mediate their differences and as leverage to argue for what each parent wants.

Lack of Focus on the Children

The third reason Child Specialists are not hired for a collaborative divorce is that parents may be unable or unwilling to put their kids' needs front and center. The presence of a CS as the advocate for the children's best interests tends to drag parents off their entrenched positions in favor of their higher values. At times, this is no picnic for parents as it indirectly requires distinguishing which negative motivations, "stories," and interpretations about the other parent are rooted in fear, the desire to be "right," or the need to "look good" in the eyes of the kids, family, and friends. Aligning behavior with values also requires differentiating negative narratives about one's co-parent from valid, reality-based fears and concerns for one's wellbeing and that of the children. Some parents are simply unwilling or unable to do or tolerate the kind of self-reflection that such work requires.

Helping Yourself and Your Kids Now

> *"When in deep water, become a diver."*
> *Ralph Blum*

There is little wisdom in waiting until you are entrenched in the divorce process to engage the multiple challenges before you. Here are some ways to help yourself and your children right now.

1. *Choose a way to divorce that preserves your assets, as well as the dignity and respect of your restructuring family.*

Deciding on the process you'll use to divorce is the single most important decision you will make. The process you choose determines how your divorce will impact your family emotionally, relationally, financially, and legally. Avoid the extra layers of pain and fear that arise from the mean-spirited, expensive, litigated courtroom battles that limit co-parents' communication to speaking only through their adversarial attorneys. Collaborative Divorce and enhanced mediation use collaboratively trained professionals who facilitate effective communication between co-parents and set the tone for co-parenting in the years ahead. You and your children can be spared years of tension, anxiety, and guilt. With collaborative divorce, you as co-parents, not attorneys or a judge, take the lead and decide what is best for your family.

Many divorce professionals say they are "collaborative," although they do not belong to a collaborative practice group or to the collaborative professional organizations that guide collaborative practice at the county, state, and international levels. "Collaborative in spirit" is *very different from being explicitly trained in collaborative divorce protocols to*:

a) Avoid adversarial legal/vernacular language usage that arises out of the win-lose, litigation model of divorce (e.g. "the parties," "the respondent," "custody agreement," "opposing counsel"). Litigation language can create an adversarial process regardless of a professional's intentions;

b) Work effectively on multidisciplinary teams by knowing and respecting the distinct professional roles, ethics, and boundaries of team members; and

c) Facilitate and honor the co-parents' right to determine their family's outcomes, while empowering them to make informed decisions and to protect the dignity and wellbeing of *all* family members.

2. *Grow intentionally.*

Instead of shrinking into bitterness, blame, or judgment, intend to use this life crisis to allow yourself to open and grow—for your sake and for your kids. Bitterness and blame have a strong, ongoing pull for us before, during, and after a divorce. Holding the intention to be open to growth takes deliberate effort and typically requires support. With that intention in mind, find a therapist who is also a collaboratively trained Divorce Coach, Child Specialist, and co-parenting specialist.

Therapy is nothing more or less than taking a class in yourself —in how you relate to yourself, and consequently, to others. The Collaborative Divorce Coaches and Child Specialist on your divorce team cannot also serve as your therapists. More than ever before, seeking individual therapy may be essential for your children and for you. Because of the inordinate stress of divorce, divorcing parents typically need extra support to think through and process their shifting lives and relationships and to transition powerfully through this challenging phase.

When choosing an independent therapist for yourself or your children, consider selecting one who is also trained in collaborative divorce and familiar with the intricacies of the divorce process. With that training, your therapist can guide you through more of the emotional and practical challenges of the divorce maze. A therapist who is also a CS can shed light on your children's divorce-related needs and help solidify your connection with them during this stressful time. You can transition more powerfully through this phase by learning the skills needed to envision and live into a future that is worthy of you and your children.

Many parents put their children in therapy before telling them about an imminent divorce. This ensures they have an established therapeutic relationship to fall back on when they are told about the divorce. As "therapy is no more than a class in your self," I suggest that parents tell children that therapy is simply a critical part of their education. To be successful and content with their lives, children have an advantage the earlier they begin learning to self-reflect, build interpersonal skills, and invest in their relationship concerns. These kids are better equipped to navigate the interpersonal challenges of school, college, and future employment.

Putting the kids in therapy *after* you tell them you are divorcing is still a very positive step, but expect to give them ample time to build a therapeutic relationship before they share themselves freely with a therapist. If kids are already in therapy when parents tell them about the divorce, a therapist (especially one trained in collaborative divorce) is better able to guide parents and prepare them to effectively address the children's specific divorce-related concerns, as well as the ongoing socio-emotional and developmental issues your children may find challenging.

Divorce is a very real opportunity to reflect on the choices and mistakes you've made and your contributions to the ending of your relationship. In addition, this is a time to develop the relationship skills you need to mindfully choose and nurture a new relationship going forward. Divorce is also a chance to re-evaluate your parenting skills, to build missing skills and the new skills needed for single-parenthood, or for step-parenting.

3. *Protect your kids from the fall-out of divorce.*

For your children, the divorce is happening at a time that impacts both their identity development and their view of what intimate relationships are like. When you divorce, your children are losing what has been true of their lives thus far — a two-parent family. They are also losing the future they expected as a given. Too often, kids are aware of all the psychodrama behind the scenes; their bodies are tense and their hearts are broken. Your words and actions toward your co-parent seriously impact your children's academic, psychological, and interpersonal effectiveness during the divorce and throughout the rest of their lives. Above all else, your children need to know that you are not divorcing them, that you both still love them, and that you will work together in a civil way, i.e. mindful of the co-parenting interactions you are modeling for them as you all move forward.

Your job as a parent is to reduce the amount of trauma and to limit the wounds and instability your children experience, so they are free to take on their own developmental challenges. Keep your problems with your co-parent to yourself. This is not the time to use your kids as buddies or allies, pretending they are unaffected by this boundary violation. You need adult friends and therapists for that support. In a Collaborative Divorce, the Child Specialist helps you ensure the kids are not pulled into the middle of your adult concerns and interests.

Make transitions between households easy for your kids. If you need to limit opportunities for negative interactions with your co-parent, there are several ways to do this. Help the kids learn how to have their own bags and school materials ready, and write or email any critical information to your co-parent before pick-up time (e.g. prescriptions, homework/school information, extracurricular information). You do all this for your children—not your co-parent. The more your kids learn to prepare and transition themselves confidently and the more fully informed your co-parent is, the more stress-free your kids can be. When your co-parent comes to pick-up the children, meditate briefly before opening the door. Be respectful and civil. Keep your goodbyes warm, calm, and short. Your anxiety becomes their anxiety, instinctively. Telling the kids you'll miss them just makes them feel guilty for leaving you. If your co-parent lingers after your goodbyes and there's a risk of exposing your kids to conflict, tension, or grief, move to a distant part of the house.

4. Speak well of your co-parent.

> "The flipside of guilt is unwillingness to forgive others. If I do not forgive myself, I do not forgive others. If I do not forgive others, I do not forgive myself. The journey is the process of letting go. Surrender!" Rita Benson

Remember, how your kids hear you speak to and about your co-parent is likely to be the pattern they follow with their own future spouses and how they will speak to that spouse in front of your future grandchildren. Your children *know* that the parent you're devaluing and rejecting is also a *part of them*. To spare your children, get whatever professional support you need to manage your frustration, anger, and sorrow. In the long run, you will earn your kids' trust with your restraint and protection.

5. *Generate faith and hope—for yourself and your kids.*

> *"You gain strength, courage and confidence by every experience in which you really stop to look fear in the face. You are able to say to yourself, 'I have lived through this horror. I can take the next thing that comes along.' You must do the thing you think you cannot do."*
> *Eleanor Roosevelt*

Rather than faith requiring absolute belief in positive outcomes, faith is simply an alternative to fear and anxiety about what you *cannot know*. Let your anxiety be your cue to remember that you can stand in faith just as easily as fear: Either way, you can't know the future. Faith is an opportunity to shift your focus intentionally towards what you want to create for yourself, your kids and your new lives. When you cannot know what's coming, you might as well stand in faith, a positive context for what *may be possible* and *aim your attention and efforts there.* Fear involves living in anticipatory misery over the countless terrible things that *might* happen. Co-parents naturally mull over the seemingly infinite unknowns of divorce, which generates more fear and anxiety—our thoughts dictate most of our feelings.

"All is well. One thing at a time" is a soothing mantra for many divorcing co-parents. Will you always *feel* like "all was well?" No! You will need some circumscribed time to be with your less positive feelings. At the same time, when your life is being turned upside down by divorce, ongoing deliberate attention will help you turn your mind and efforts back to focus on what you wish to create for yourself and your kids. Reassure yourself with gratitude for ways of being you ordinarily take for granted—e.g. you are loving and loved, you are healthy and well, you have a roof over your head, food on the table, and a way to get around. Gratitude generates faith and optimism. Keep reminding yourself about what you "love and are grateful for"—your kids are healthy and loved, for example. Remind yourself of the specific people you can call on in a pinch. You can attend to neglected job skills, your business, making your new living space feel like home, etc.

During my own divorce, I wrote out similar reassurances as well as inspiring quotes on sticky notes and put them by the toilet, on my computer, my dashboard, my nightstand, and bathroom mirror. I made a daily practice of listing 10 ways of being or things that "Today, I love and am grateful for," and shared the list with friends, who shared theirs with me. I surrounded myself with friends and professionals I trusted to help me acknowledge and keep building on all my strengths.

Amidst all the inevitable losses of divorce, divorce *is* a beginning. Slowly but surely, your new life emerges. Most co-parents are fairly effective advocates for others. As you wade through the quagmire of divorce challenges, you have the opportunity, especially with effective professional support, to become a powerful advocate *for* yourself (not *against* your co-parent), strategically creating the love and life you want going forward. Furthermore, Chloe Neill affirms that: "The best revenge is a life well lived." When you generate faith and hope, you are more likely to create and live into what's possible for yourself, your children, and your future. I have seen this kind of rebirth happen repeatedly for parents and children of all ages, in all circumstances.

Divorce can be a time of rebirth when you are willing to deliberately engage and learn its lessons. If I were to win the lottery, I would still do this deeply satisfying work to bear witness to the reliable miracles of growth. It is my privilege and honor to facilitate the optimism, love, compassion, and skills that allow the human spirit to soar in trying circumstances.

Having a Collaborative Child Specialist on your collaborative divorce team will help you ensure that your children's best interests and wellbeing remain central throughout the divorce process, while helping to protect them from the inevitable fall-out. Guided by your highest values as parents, an effective CS will advocate and give voice to your kids' needs throughout this challenging family transition. With a collaborative divorce, it is possible for your family to restructure with healthier, post-divorce roles and interactions than existed before.

❖

For free resources on *specifics* about how to use gratitude to move from anxious overwhelm to creativity and grace, how to make the process easier on your kids, how to tell your children about your divorce, and much more, visit RiaSeverance. com.

Key Takeaways

✓ Divorce is a traumatic life crisis, full of uncertainties for most families. However, there are a number ways to spare your kids a lifetime of ongoing parental strife and tension.

✓ Collaborative Divorce, unlike any other divorce model, provides for a neutral Child Specialist to advocate for and to ensure the kids' best interests and wellbeing remain at the forefront of all divorce-related decisions.

✓ The child-centered concerns of all other team members risk being treated as unsolicited intrusions by overwhelmed co-parents; the CS is the only team member with an exclusive mandate to protect and advocate for the children.

✓ As "the voice of the children" and guided by parents' highest values, the CS empowers Collaborative Divorce Coaches to help co-parents develop a relationship that can effectively engage their children's unique needs.

✓ Collaborative Divorce is designed to encourage growth, to facilitate the aligning of your co-parenting behavior with your highest values, and, to not only protect your children, but to support your creating a future in which both you and your children can thrive.

ABOUT RIA SEVERANCE, LMFT

Ria Severance is a Licensed Marriage and Family Therapist in private practice. She also serves as a Collaborative Divorce Coach, Child Specialist, Co-Mediator, Co-Parenting Specialist, and Executive Development Consultant.

Drawing from her work with 100s of children and parents, Ms. Severance helps families stay out of court by empowering separating or divorcing parents to develop a parenting plan and form an alliance and skill set that puts the best interests of children first, while addressing the needs of *all* family members.

Ria offers a variety of therapy options to assist parents at various points in the divorce process, including: Decision Counseling to determine whether to divorce, Couples Counseling, in-home Parent Coaching for parents dealing with their children's behavioral challenges, Co-Parent Training, and divorce-related Individual Therapy to work through divorce challenges while creating a new life.

A bilingual/bicultural Latina, Ms. Severance has 30 years of clinical experience developing relationships with people of diverse cultures, classes, interests and needs. She is a dynamic speaker and offers monthly free trainings in Pasadena, California, for clinicians and the public regarding the pros and cons of different divorce options. Ria also provides professional trainings at annual conferences for Collaborative Practice California (CP Cal) and the International Association of Collaborative Professionals (IACP).

Ms. Severance is active as the Marketing Chair for Pasadena Collaborative Divorce, a Board Member for Los Angeles Collaborative Family Law Association

(LACFLA), a Founding Member and Marketing and Training Committee Member for Civil Collaborative Professionals, and she also volunteers as a Co-Mediator and Divorce Coach at Loyola Law School.

BUSINESS NAME: Ria Severance, LMFT
WEBSITE: www.riaseverance.com
EMAIL: ria@riaseverance.com
PHONE: 626-354-4334
LOCATION: South Pasadena, CA

A New True North: Navigating a Path with Your Divorce Coach to Your New Understanding of Family

by Dominique Walmsley, MA, LMHC

"If you want to build a ship, don't drum up people together to collect wood and don't assign them tasks and work, but rather teach them to long for the endless immensity of the sea."
-Antoine de Saint-Exupery

Divorce clearly has legal and practical components; however, it also has an emotional part that is often hidden because of the way we think about emotions as weaknesses. Emotions can be disruptive to thinking. They often bring to our attention something we might not want to see or tell anyone—a deeper truth about ourselves. Sometimes, the emotions bring conflict within us.

Collaborative Law helps resolve those emotional binds, makes space to address them, allows people to feel safe to bring them up, and has a plan for working them out. Including your emotions in the divorce process can make all the difference in ensuring a healthier process for all involved. The divorce coach is the emotional professional on the Collaborative Law team. When the team is utilized fully and participants work through the process until all issues are satisfactorily resolved, the outcome of a Collaborative Law divorce can be expected to include the following emotional benefits.

Relationship with Self (Your Inner World)

1. Recovery to Normalization

- You won't feel threatened. You will not experience sudden strong and unexpected emotions (also known as triggers) about the process after the divorce. You won't have fears about your ability to do those things to which you agreed. Your guilt and regrets have been discussed, internalized, understood, and have evolved into understanding and appropriate remorse, disappointment, or grief.

- You feel emotionally capable. You can assess your urges to display anger, and with appropriate effort, calm them by your own meaning system under which you created the divorce agreement. You will be able to manage your urges to pull the children into disagreements ("badmouthing") with your ex because you can talk to him or her directly.

- You feel grounded. You can help other family members regain grounding.

2. Self-Confidence

- You have the skills and the ability to advocate for your well-being. A good divorce process will be able to restore the self-confidence you might have lost leading up to the divorce decision. For you to do well at work and with your family, you need confidence and trust in yourself.

- You need to be able to speak to your ex, your children, and even a new spouse with confidence when you have assessed that conversation is needed for the well-being of family members.

3. Absence of Trauma from the Process Itself

- When you look back after your divorce, you will think that the process you chose was fair and addressed your interests. You will have a sense that the process supported your financial, social, and emotional recovery.

- Addressing trauma triggers by getting help, support, comfort, or understanding is normal for recovery. When tracking the triggers over time, you will notice that they are diminishing.

Relationship with Others (Your Outer World)

4. Continued Cooperation Within Your Family System

- Every family member works together to settle difficulties. Difficulties that do come up will be solved easily. People will feel interconnected and can access empathy and understanding for each other in the ups and downs of life. The family system includes grown children, extended family, friends, and other shared social relationships.

5. Children Are Open with and Confide in Both Parents in Developmentally Healthy Ways

- The natural and instinctual loyalty that children feel towards their parents is not hampered by their fear of hurting the other parent or by their fear of protesting against a parent. They can push back in developmentally appropriate ways without parents feeling afraid of their connection.

A skilled divorce coach provides the necessary support for divorcing couples to separate while also redeveloping their relationship as co-parents and integrating their extended families and friends. Coaches will monitor the emotional components of the divorce and actively guide participants through important discussions.

Experiencing Ambivalence and the Unknown

Most often people are ambivalent about getting divorced because, deep down, there are aspects they still like about being married. Divorcing takes courage. It takes a commitment. You know that the marriage is making you feel worse and probably act worse than you'd like. Choosing to divorce is often a desperate act. You are going to break down the place that should be the safest in a world—the home. Your children will have to find a new home-place and may not always be able to make sense of the world while they are adjusting.

That inner conflict causes ambivalence. Most often one person comes to the conclusion to divorce, while the other still has hope for the relationship. Or they might be unsuccessful being amicable during the process, even if they vowed to do so. They don't realize how damaging the process can be to their future relationship, and even though they try hard, they cannot always keep the painful emotions suppressed. It is sad to see that the process itself can be so harmful.

One couple, Mary and Joe, didn't talk through their parenting plan, thinking that the children were old enough and that Mary, always the primary parent, could work it out herself. Joe didn't care much at the time anyway. After the divorce, Joe remarried and began to have an interest in spending time with the children, now in high school and college. They no longer had support from the team to guide them through the process of including Joe's wishes. Mary was resistant to change now, so long after the process, and the children were angry, not understanding the reasons. Mary was suspicious about the new wife's intentions, but there was no method for integrating her into the divorced family. There were still loose ends, and working through these brought back the painful memories of their disagreements before the divorce. Mary became depressed, and Joe became angry in a very passive way, pulling the children into the conversations. Emotions showed up. A good divorce would have caught the unfinished business of Joe being dismissive and Mary feeling unresolved about how hard she had worked to stimulate his interest in his children and to protect the children from being drawn back into the process emotionally.

To make a simplistic statement, we could say that emotions have a mind of their own. They show up. And they speak. Recognizing their power and accepting that they need to have a voice, Collaborative Law divorces make room for working through the issues that have emotional power. The Collaborative Law process sets the stage for a more amicable process. The attorneys have agreed to work together for the good of everyone in the family. The team signs the participation agreement which outlines boundaries that have been carefully tested to give couples the best chance of using emotions well to support deliberations. The divorce coach, an expert in emotions, tracks the deliberations and reminds people to include the emotions.

When the team of professionals shares their information and impressions with each other, they have a common knowledge base about the couples that helps increase the likelihood of a positive outcome. This information includes the visible and the invisible aspects of divorce—the house and finances as well as the emotions of the children and the heirlooms that have personal value. At the beginning of the process, the team and the couple make a list of things to discuss. Some are easy and can be resolved simply. Others are not so easy. The team can help by providing paths to resolutions by offering resources: education about what needs to be known, forms and protocols for working out problems, and other professional neutrals who can guide and support the couples in making decisions.

And then there are the emotional issues—the ones that make people feel angry, insecure, misunderstood, entitled, sad, or helpless. To put those aside is ultimately impossible. Emotional issues come back like pesky little bugs, showing up in unsatisfying, intrusive, irritating, and debilitating ways. They are the legacy of an incomplete divorce. So how can one better understand what is going on and then work these out? How can one do a complete divorce? What else is needed?

Until now, people expected that, if you are an adult, you should just deal with emotions on your own. But what if they are the result of a traumatic response? What if those emotions have something useful to say, but we are not listening to them? What if we have the wrong idea of what those emotions mean? If they are misunderstood and dismissed, they will come back in embarrassing ways and be shamed into submission.

Experiencing Emotions in Conflict

One of the central aims of a good outcome is to manage the conflict between the individuals going through the process. Understanding the origins of this conflict helps to reduce it. The tendency to shame those who argue or show anger or despair is counterproductive because the feelings have a life of their own, as we have already seen. By understanding emotional conflict, as described in this chapter, conflict naturally diminishes.

Emotions inform us about the world and help us to navigate a safe journey through life. They are not the enemy. Feeling fearful in a dark jungle reminds us that we need to be careful of animals that could kill us. As humans, we are used to managing our emotions in public, and we forget they serve a good purpose. Remembering this can help decode the emotions that arise throughout the divorce process. What, then, is the purpose of emotions in divorce?

At the outset of a divorce, you know the safety of the home is going to change. Hopefully, you will find a new way to be safe, but no one knows how things will evolve before the discussions have occurred. There are hopes and expectations, but these still need to be negotiated. Another common emotion concerns the pain that others, such as children, have to suffer because of the divorce. Some good things end, even when divorce is the best overall approach. The passage of time eases the pain, as does having a good outcome.

To have an amicable divorce, all of these potential threats to a good future must be resolved. Because they are not all concrete issues, they might keep rumbling underneath the visible world. Emotional issues are often due to feelings or senses about what might not be going well, and these might be difficult to articulate.

New research has shown that our bodies participate in the generation of emotions and that there is a strong connection between the body and the brain. Stephen Porges developed *Polyvagal Theory* based on his findings. In *The Healing Power of Emotion*[12], he writes:

> To survive, mammals must determine friend from foe and when an environment is safe, and they must be able to communicate to their social unit. These survival-related behaviors limit the extent to which a mammal can be physically approached, whether vocalizations will be understood, and whether coalitions can be established. Moreover, these behavioral strategies, which are used to navigate through the "stress of life," form the bedrock upon which social behaviors and higher cognitive processes can be developed and expressed. Thus, learning and other expansive mental processes must be structured, manipulated, and studied within the context of how the environment fosters or ameliorates stress-related physiological states. (p. 36).

Science is backing up the long-held view that emotions are here to stay and that they are meant to be useful guides toward a fuller and more satisfying human existence.

Emotional stresses cannot be resolved by just determining not to show emotions during the mediation discussions, during the move out from home,

---

[12]. *Porges, S. (2009). Reciprocal Influences Between Body and Brain in the Perception and Expression of Affect: A Polyvagal Perspective. In D. Fosha, D. Siegel & M. Solomon (Eds.) The Healing Power of Emotions. New York, NY: Norton*

or when telling the children. *Polyvagal Theory* shows that the stress associated with divorce needs to be addressed. The changes brought on by divorce are challenging to our instincts and our system of mind and body. If they are not resolved during the process, people will potentially have a lot of work to do afterward. This can be difficult when you don't have good access to your partner anymore. A Collaborative Law approach can better prepare you for life after the divorce and for effectively and safely working through these emotions.

Level of Threat

When we feel good, our emotional system and our thinking system are balanced. Both are functioning optimally. When our senses are alerted to something threatening, that balance is disturbed because our survival is threatened. Automatically, our bodies prepare for escape. Our deliberative system that usually thinks and plans carefully is put on standby as our bodies prepare to fight or run away. In the divorce process, if it seems like our partners are not listening to us about things that are very important, we switch into coping styles, those methods we use when we don't feel safe. For example, we may fight harder to force people into listening and obeying, or we retreat and hope for the best. Once the threat is attended to and resolved, we get a deep sense of peace, and our functioning becomes guided by a clear mind. When the level of threat is high and remains unattended to, we can feel overwhelmed. Our survival needs must be met first.

Feelings of safety and connection are essential for good functioning. If either person starts using coping mechanisms, these must be addressed in the process. Additionally, the survival needs must be addressed before people can get out of conflict mode and into collaboration. Relying on the divorce coach to track intense emotions is very useful when desiring a good outcome that is sustainably healthy. Being open about your concerns and fears is important and lets the coach know your vulnerabilities. If you are afraid to open up about these, you can get help with that, too. It might not feel safe for you when you fear that your partner will shut down or get angry. However, putting all of those issues on the table when you are with the coach will allow you to get the support you need.

With the help of a divorce coach, Amy and Frank did just that. Both had new partners. Frank knew Amy's partner and trusted him. Amy had not met Frank's partner yet. Their son, Alex, was five years old. One day, as planned, Frank swung by Amy's house to pick up some furniture. Amy had told Alex that he would see his daddy for a quick hello, but that didn't happen. Due to this misunderstanding, there was a lot of tension in the next meeting with the attorneys, where they planned to discuss financial matters. Amy and Frank were timid and angry. The attorneys advised them to come for a session with me, their coach. Through discussion about their emotions and intentions in the safety of my office, it came to light that Amy didn't trust Frank because he had acted strangely and unexpectedly and had hurt Alex. Frank was then able to admit to the distress he experienced that day with his new partner and his need to support her in her emotional swings. He had been somewhat ashamed of his new partner's emotional challenges, but through my assurances and understanding was able to notice that Amy could accept his challenges with his new partner. Frank could then be more open with Amy if he had a need to be with his new partner instead of taking the time to give Alex a quick hello and a hug.

Experiencing Interconnectedness

Because we are social creatures, we want connection and need it to feel good. Sensing a break in an established connection makes us anxious and will register below our awareness, in our unconscious. We have empathy, which means that we feel *with* other people. We can now even measure empathy in the brain. Hooked up to electrodes to measure brain activity, one primate showed activation in the empathy center of the brain when his trainer hurt himself on his way out of the lab. Even at a distance, a primate could feel the pain of the trainer. How much more so would a divorcing person experience the emotional distress of a partner, even one whom he or she is divorcing? How much more would a child, even if parents didn't argue in front of him or her, notice that there is distress or emotional pain in the air?

At my urging, Jenny and Francis (who had a 10-year-old daughter named Amanda) took a risk and invited Francis's new partner Sandra to a coaching session. Francis stayed home. Sandra and Jenny were then able to talk about their approaches to parenting Amanda. Though tense in the first session, they reported at their second session that their discussion had brought new insight about each other, and their fears about going to events where both would be present had completely subsided. They also reported greater ability to hear Amanda's positive and negative comments about the other.

Normally, they would not have had such a discussion on their own. However, with my knowledge of them and about emotions that arise in family separations, during the session, I could see that there was a great likelihood that it would resolve a lot of their confusion and lack of confidence about each other. A face-to-face meeting often reduces interpersonal distress. This happens so often that I often suggest it to couples and co-parents.

Experiencing Attachment: Family Does Not Go Away

Attachment Theory for adults, which was developed through observation of people in distress, has supported a lot of robust work in healing conflict and emotional pain. Researchers Mario Mikulincer and Phillip Shaver, authors of *Attachment in Adulthood*[13], show that we are hard-wired for relationships. We are relational beings through and through.

The bonding that occurs between people is not only a feel-good moment, but it also has an impact on our bodies, our arousal system, our emotions, and on our sense of who we are. The responsiveness of adults to helpless newborns sets a pattern in the children's brains that helps them know when things are not safe. Through their caregivers, they recognize that the world helps them (or not), and they develop capacities to respond accordingly. Some people are constantly vigilant even though there is no threat because they might have spent their formative years in an environment where they got no help.

Bonding between family members is going to have a reverberating effect during and after divorce. In my practice, grown individuals whose parents divorced decades ago feel pain in their lives because of that divorce. In the initial therapy session when I ask about their reasons for coming, one of the first things they tell me is the age at which their parents divorced. Even children who were grown when their parents divorced go through painful adjustments. Pretending that we can cut off a relationship will only perpetuate the emotional pain longer and possibly cause conflict, which results from that bond being broken unmindfully. Acknowledging the emotions that we now know are generated by a bond being threatened or broken will allow the emotions to come into view and be reworked. Adults and their children can then go forward without the ongoing reactivity and negative feelings when their exes come to mind or show up at family gatherings.

Because we care about our children in an instinctual way, we will feel intense feelings if we think their wellbeing is threatened, even if it is only when they miss us at night at the home of the other parent. These fears need to be adjusted. Just hoping that they will heal with time might leave more work to do later.

Even if you choose to divorce amicably, it is best to assume that children will be affected so that you can keep an eye on them with that in mind. You will then be able to assist in their recovery, if necessary, knowing that they are suffering because of the trauma and not merely due to childhood development.

---

[13]. *Mikulincer, M. & Shaver, P. (2010). Attachment in Adulthood: Structure, Dynamics, and Change. New York, NY: Guilford.*

Experiencing Divorce as Trauma

The way in which emotions suddenly show up so strongly that they seem unbearable, either because of something you think or because you see something in the environment that triggers you, is a trauma response. Divorce is highly likely to be traumatic. As you have just read, attachment is primary, and when it is shaky or insecure, a reaction will be set in motion that involves the arousal system and the emotions. As a result, you might suddenly feel like you did during a threatening moment in the past. This is a form of PTSD, where something triggers a strong emotion more intense than the situation warrants. Framing divorce as trauma helps us understand why it is known to include painful arguments and known to affect children negatively.

Allan Schore, a trauma specialist and researcher, speaks to the value of considering trauma in *The Healing Power of Emotion*[14]. "Overwhelming traumatic feelings that are not regulated cannot be adaptively integrated into the patient's emotional life. This dissociative deficit specifically results from a lack of integration of the right hemisphere, the emotional brain" (p. 140).

If the emotional part is integrated into the divorce process, the brain can manage emotions. In that way, we can be consistent in our mood and our presentation of ourselves or, as Schore says, we can allow "for a continuity of inner experience" (p. 141). This continuity and steadiness are crucial in divorce deliberations. Being able to be steady also regulates your partner's emotions, keeping him or her in a fit state to negotiate. Emotions of loss, regret, and fear of the unknown will show up.

Carol's husband had an affair and then an ongoing relationship with the affair partner. For a long time after she separated from him, she couldn't allow herself to let their son spend the night at his father's house if the new partner was going to be there. The painful feelings of this new partner having been, in Carol's mind, so seductive as to cause the betrayal by her husband, at the expense of her child, slowed down her ability to accept that her son would be safe in his father's home. She said about him, "He is not the man I married." This kind of comment indicates to me that the bond was not properly evolved into a post-divorce co-parenting bond in which she could trust him at a distance. It took many coaching sessions to regain her self-confidence.

---

14. *Schore, A. Right Brain Affect Regulation: An Essential Mechanism of Development, Trauma, Dissociation, and Psychotherapy. In D. Fosha, D. Siegel, & M. Solomon (Eds.). The Healing Power of Emotion. New York, NY: Norton.*

A Good Outcome

Emotions are going to surface because they assess how well the world suits us at any time. Emotions are our friends. They surface because divorce threatens our safe place. Divorce also requires us to make a new safe place, and in that way, it requires that we do certain tasks. The fragile ones for whom we are responsible, namely our children, rely on our assessment of safety, both for them and for ourselves. We need to be stable, and they need to sense that we are safe in order for them to trust the world. They see the world through our eyes. For older children and extended family members, our emotions give information about how safe and stable we are—maybe even how happy we are and whether we are available to them in the way they know us. Stabilizing emotions will give us a better chance to fulfill those tasks. People naturally care about each other and will be affected, even if they are trying not to care.

A good outcome of the divorce process is one in which everyone can make the transition to the restructured family thoughtfully and deliberatively. The goal is to remain or become psychologically intact, to have energy for the future, and to be able to be relational without restrictions to all members of the original family. The relationship with self and the relationship with others should both be healthy, and the settlement should feel fair and maintain a fair platform for everyone to go forward in their lives. Because growth takes time, there will most likely be a period of transition in which the outcomes are not fully manifested, but after the transition, the Collaborative Law process can bring about the desired outcomes.

❖

Contact Dominique via email (dominique@seattlemindcounseling.com) for the key to calming down emotionally charged conversations with techniques that are scientifically significant and enduring.

Key Takeaways

✓ Divorce can be a traumatic process with long-term negative effects–most pointedly, emotional effects.

✓ Finding a professional who can help you understand and work through the emotional challenges will have lasting effects in your and your family's life.

✓ The level of threat felt by either partner going through any part of the divorce process will affect the decisions being made. They may be momentary solutions based on temporary emotions. Emotions are not easily seen or understood, and may be working below consciousness.

✓ Making your own decisions and coming to agreements that you both know will be best for your family is better than allowing anyone else to make those decisions for you or making them when you feel strong negative emotions.

✓ The Collaborative Law process is designed to help you in the process of making your own decisions.

ABOUT DOMINIQUE WALMSLEY, MA, LMHC

Dominique Walmsley is a Collaborative Law Coach, Child Specialist, and Psychotherapist practicing in Seattle, Washington. She is currently pursuing her doctorate and doing research on the divorce process. Her interest is to increase the human experience in the divorce process and help people resolve their conflicts to bring about greater harmony in their post-divorce relationships. In her practice, she specializes in couple therapy in all aspects of the life cycle and is especially interested in the existential approach and recovery from trauma.

Dominique began her career as an architect. At the time, she was a Dutch citizen living in South Africa. She has three grown children and has cultivated rich life experiences that contribute to her wisdom in helping people move through stuck places into a greater sense of freedom. Her ultimate goal is to the assist her clients to live life to the fullest, both as individuals and as family members.

BUSINESS NAME: Seattle Mind Counseling
WEBSITE: www.seattlemindcounseling.com
EMAIL: dominique@seattlemindcounseling.com
PHONE: (206) 909-1097
LOCATION: Seattle, WA

www.ingramcontent.com/pod-product-compliance
Lightning Source LLC
LaVergne TN
LVHW051420080426
835508LV00022B/3176